Notes On Neotropical Dragonflies, Or Odonata... - Primary Source Edition

Edward Bruce Williamson

NOTES ON NEOTROPICAL DRAGONFLIES, OR ODONATA.

By Edward Bruce Williamson,
Of Bluffton, Indiana.

These notes consist of four brief papers relating to agrionines of the genera *Metaleptobasis*, *Palaemnema*, *Telagrion*, and *Protoneura*. While these four papers are distinct and of different charactors, it is believed that their publication under one general head will be found to be convenient. The Guatemala material was collected by myself; that from British Guiana and Trinidad by my father, L. A. Williamson, B. J. Rainey, and myself.

1. THREE NEW SPECIES OF METALEPTOBASIS.

As *Metaleptobasis* is now understood [1] less than a dozen specimens have been described or mentioned in the literature relating to the several species. On March 8, 1912, my father, L. A. Williamson, and I were collecting at a small swamp about 1¾ miles west of Cumuto, Trinidad, on the north side of and immediately adjacent to the railroad track. This is a small swamp, near the railroad, surrounded by higher ground, full of logs and grass, and containing fish and alligators. The larger part of the swamp near the railroad is exposed to the sun, and this portion of the swamp apparently has resulted from the fill for the railroad grade. Back from the railroad the swamp is interspersed with small thickets which shade the ground, and at the extreme upper portion it ends in woods through which a small and very muddy creek flows into the swamp. In the afternoon, after several hours at the swamp, we detected for the first time a slender dragonfly in grass, and clinging to small twigs and vines just at the border or slightly back from the border of the swamp and in the shade. Having once found it we could hardly believe we had overlooked it during the earlier part of the day. But a short time could be spent that day looking for them but we succeeded in taking 18 males. Wishing to get females and more specimens Mr. B. J. Rainey and I returned to the swamp on March 10, 1912, and spent the day there. In addition to many other things we took 52

[1] Calvert, Philip P. Biologia Centrali-Americana, Odonata, p, 386, November, 1907; Contributions to a knowledge of the Odonata of the Neotropical Region, exclusive of Mexico and Central America, Ann. Carnegie Mus., vol. 6, No. 1, p. 197, October 7, 1909.

males of *Metaleptobasis*, but neither of us were able to find the females, though we went some distance into the woods in several directions. When papering this material a unique male of a very distinct species was detected; and later study of the collection reveals another species, represented by 3 males. This last species is also represented by a single male from British Guiana. Thus of the 70 specimens of *Metaleptobasis* taken about this little swamp in Trinidad, 66 belong to a species (*manicaria*) not known elsewhere; 3 belong to a very closely related species (*mauritia*) known also from British Guiana; and the unique (*brysonima*) is more closely related to *bovilla*, known from Guatemala and Nicaragua, than to any other species. In this connection attention may be called to the fact that 2 species of the genus were added to the known dragonfly fauna of Trinidad by our efforts in collecting a very large series of what, at the time, we presumed was one species. Moreover, on the second day Mr. Rainey collected a unique male of another genus, which would not have been found but for his careful search for *Metaleptobasis*.

METALEPTOBASIS BOVILLA Calvert.

Hitherto known from a single male from Nicaragua and a single female from Guatemala. The female is in my collection. The capture of another male in Guatemala indicates that Doctor Calvert was correct in associating the 2 specimens before him. I caught this male on June 23, 1909, in the swampy palm woods on the left side (as one approaches Puerto Barrios) of the railroad track just back from Puerto Barrios. It was clinging to a vine several feet from the ground. No others were seen, but the careful search, which later experience has shown necessary, was not made.

METALEPTOBASIS BRYSONIMA,[1] new species.

Related to *M. bovilla* and described in the tabulations which follow. It may be separated at once from *bovilla* by the form of the abdominal appendages which are figured for both species.

The following notes were made on the living colors: Eyes bright green beneath, above very dark green in front, with a large posterior red spot (this refers to the dorsal surface of the eyes), the green and red separated by a triangular black area, one side of the triangle being against the vertex. Dorsum of thorax narrowly metallic black, on either side dark flesh red, shading out to paler below and behind. Dorsum of abdomen black, sides dull yellowish; about apical half of 7 and all of 8–10 about the color of the mesepimeron (flesh red).

Described from a single male in my collection taken March 10, 1912, at the swamp described above near Cumuto, Trinidad.

[1] As in the following two species, I am under obligations to Mr. W. E. Broadway, of the Botanic Station, Tobago, who has kindly furnished me with three generic names of plants which occur in the savannahs near Cumuto and elsewhere in Trinidad. *Brysonima* is "a small scraggy-looking tree characteristic of these natural savannahs."

METALEPTOBASIS MAURITIA,[1] new species.

Related to the following species from which it is most readily separated by the shorter abdominal appendages and the form of the apex of abdominal segment 10. Described in the tabulations which follow from 4 specimens in my collection, 3 males from the swamp near Cumuto, Trinidad, March 10, 1912; and 1 male from near Tumatumari, Potaro River, British Guiana, February 9, 1912. This last male was collected in a low, flat area on the right bank of the river just above Tumatumari. On this date this flat was dry, but it showed evidence of being frequently submerged for long periods. The ground was bare over large portions of the surface, and the vegetation was in scattered clumps, confined to a very few species. The dragonfly was taken resting on a leaf near the ground. More careful and intelligent search might have revealed more, but only the one was seen. While the specimen from British Guiana is considerably larger than the Trinidad specimens, I am convinced that they are the same species. The type of *mauritia* is a male from Trinidad, in my collection.

Paratype.—Cat. No. 18063, U.S.N.M. One of the 3 males from Cumuto, Trinidad, mentioned above.

METALEPTOBASIS MANICARIA,[2] new species.

Related to *mauritia* and described in the tabulations which follow. Sixty-six males, all taken at the swamp near Cumuto, Trinidad, on March 8 and 10, 1912, are before me.

The following notes were made on the living colors: Colors generally dull. Eyes beneath light bluish green, above dark green, with a posterior bright orange spot[3] which is bordered in front with black (as in the case of *brysonima*, not only these brilliant colors of the eyes fade but the pattern even disappears). Dorsum of thorax narrowly black; mesepisternum pale greenish brown; mesepimeron paler; metepisternum and metepimeron pale yellowish with greenish reflections. Dorsum of abdomen metallic greenish black, below this bluish green, rather dull and obscured; segments 8–10 dull yellowish brown with bluish or greenish traces laterally.

Two specimens in 95 per cent alcohol, one year after capture, are as follows: The colors of the eyes are well preserved, with the orange somewhat paler. The mesepimeron, metepisternum, and metepimeron are about the same color, pale yellowish, but I do not detect the greenish reflections, which are still evident, however, on the apical

[1] *Mauritia* is the generic name of "the tall palm which grows in quantity together on the savannah" (Broadway).

[2] *Manicaria* is the generic name of "a palm which I have seen in watery positions near Cumuto" (Broadway).

[3] This spot is on the posterior portion of the dorsal surface of the eyes; not to be confused with the rear of the head or eyes.

abdominal segments. Segment 7 is apically colored like the segments following it, and on its sides the pale colors extend almost or quite to its base.

Of the total number of this species before me 3 have one mesothoracic horn incomplete or wanting. The last postnodals of 8 specimens were examined; in the front wing the last postnodal was continuous in 6 cases, not continuous in 10; in the hind wing, continuous in 3 cases, not continuous in 13 cases. The type is a male in my collection.

Paratype.—Cat. No. 18064, U.S.N.M. Four of the males from Cumuto, Trinidad, mentioned above, two of which were collected on March 8 and the other two on March 10.

METALEPTOBASIS (?), species.

In the tabulations which follow, a female probably belonging to *Metaleptobasis* is described. I believe this specimen represents an unnamed species, but, in so far as its association with the proper male of possibly several closely related species may be difficult, and as apparently in this genus males are more frequently taken than females, to name this species at this time might result in delay, annoyance, and possible confusion for subsequent authors. The specimen was taken in swampy woods near Rockstone, British Guiana, January 30, 1912.

Comparison of characters of species in the genus Metaleptobasis.

	bovilla, male.	*brysonima*, male.	*mauritia*, male.	*manicaria*, male.	*sp.*, female.
Length of abdomen (mm.).	37	34	37 (Trinidad). 41 (British Guiana)	37	33
Length of hind wing (mm.).	22	20.5	22 (Trinidad). 24 (British Guiana)	21	21
Labium....	Pale flesh; cleft in median lobe wide, U-shaped, with sides of cleft not parallel.	Flesh colored; cleft in median lobe half as wide as in *bovilla*, sides parallel.	Pale flesh; cleft in median lobe intermediate in width with two preceding species, cleft widest near the middle, sides not parallel.	Same as *mauritia*.	Pale flesh; cleft in median lobe short, wide, and rounded.
Labrum...	Shining black.	Light reddish brown, darker basally and laterally.	Brown, paler basally, lateral margins darker.	Pattern similar to *mauritia* but central area greenish brown.	Shining black.
Rhinarium.	Ultra ash gray, with a basal dark spot on either side of median line.	Very light brown with a dark spot on either side of median line.	Pale dull blue green with a dark spot on either side of median line.	Similar to *mauritia*.	Black.

Comparison of characters of species in the genus Metaleptobasis—Continued.

	bovilla, male.	*brysonima*, male.	*mauritia*, male.	*manicaria*, male.	*sp.*, female.
Nasus	Black; on anterior edge on either side is a shining black ocellus-like spot.	Similar to *bovilla*.	Dark gray, almost black, with shining black spots as in *bovilla*.	Dark and dull apple green, almost black in some cases, with shining spots as in *bovilla*.	Black.
Frons in front.	Obscure pale clay yellow.	Dark, almost black, with a blue green cast.	Obscure dull blue green.	Obscure dull blue green, very dark in some cases.	Dark, almost black, with a blue green cast.
Frons above.	Black.	Black.	Black, or nearly so.	Dark brown, almost black.	Black.
Vertex	Black, the merest trace of the orange line between the lateral ocellus and the antenna described by Calvert (Biol. Cent. Amer., p. 386).	Black.	Black, obscurely patterned with slightly paler.[1]	Black or nearly so and obscurely patterned with slightly paler.[1]	Black, with a dull orange, short, wide stripe near each eye, each stripe parallel with the rear of the head in dorsal view.
Gena	Pale dull blue green, a round dark spot opposite anterior face of frons.	Blue green, with a narrow dark bar across the gena opposite the anterior face of frons.	Blue green, a round black spot, not quite reaching the eye, opposite anterior face of frons.	Same as *mauritia*, but dark spot smaller.	Pale blue green, unspotted.
Rear of head.	Pale flesh.	Pale flesh.	Pale flesh.	Pale flesh.	Pale flesh.
Antenna	Black, second joint pale except extreme apex.	Same as *bovilla*.	Same as *bovilla*.	Same as *bovilla*.	Same, but apical half or third of second segment black.
Prothorax.	Flesh colored, darker and redder above.	Same as *bovilla*.	Same as *bovilla*, posterior lobe sometimes black.	Same as *bovilla*.	Same as *bovilla*.
Thorax	Middorsal stripe metallic green, about 0.5 mm. wide; mesepisternum brown ocher, passing ventrally and posteriorly into pale flesh color on metepimeron.	Same as *bovilla*.	Middorsal stripe black with but a trace, if any, of metallic green, about 0.5 mm. wide; mesepisternum pale brown, passing ventrally and posteriorly into pale flesh color on metepimeron.	Middorsal stripe metallic green, about 0.25 mm. wide or less, otherwise like *mauritia*.	Color of *bovilla* but no middorsal stripe; on outer half of mesepisternum and on suture between mesepimeron and metepisternum is stippling in dark reddish brown, forming 2 diffuse bands.

[1] Possibly the darkest areas on the vertex are, on either side a band running from the lateral ocellus to the eye, its outer end posterior to the antenna; and a shorter band about half as long, behind the first band, from which it is separated by about its own width, this shorter band reaching the eye; the shorter band is subparallel to the longer band anterior to it and is slightly curved, the convex side anterior, while in the longer band the convex side is posterior. These areas or bands are not always discernible. In addition a less defined dark band may sometimes be detected which extends from the inner end of the shorter band, above described, to the eye, this band being parallel to the outline of the rear of the head in dorsal view.

Comparison of characters of species in the genus Metaleptobasis—Continued.

	bovilla, male.	*brysonima*, male.	*mauritia*, male.	*manicaria*, male.	*sp.*, female.
Abdomen..	1 dark flesh colored, darker apically, 2-10 dark brown or black dorsally; pale interrupted basal rings on 3-8; sides of 8 brown, 10 largely brown, 2-6 beneath pale, darker apically, 7-10 beneath light brown.	1-7 similar to *bovilla;* 8-10 pale dull brown ocher.	1-7 similar to *bovilla;* 8-10 dull brown ocher, basal half of 9 darker; in one specimen basal three-fourths of 8 and basal three-fifths of 9 dark.	Similar to *brysonima*, but 7 apically more or less the color of 8-10.	Similar to *bovilla*, but basal rings evident only on 2 and 3.
Legs.......	Pale, tarsal claws not toothed.	Same as *bovilla*.	Same as *bovilla*.	Same as *bovilla*.	Same as *bovilla*.
Stigma.....	Covering 1 cell; dark brown, paler just against the inclosing veins.	Covering 1 cell or slightly less; brown ocher, paler just against the inclosing veins.	Not quite or covering 1 cell; pale brown, paler just against the inclosing veins.	Same as *mauritia;* generally covering 1 cell; brown, paler against the inclosing veins.	Reduced, covering much less than 1 cell; pale brown, paler just against the inclosing veins.
Cubito-anal cross vein from quadrangle.	Not over twice its own length.	About twice its own length.	Same as *brysonima*.	2-3 times its own length.	More than 3 times its own length.
Posterior wing margin meeting anal vein.	Slightly distal to cubito-anal cross vein.	Same as *bovilla*.	More distal than in the 2 preceding species; about the length of the cubito-anal cross vein or more.	Same as *bovilla*.	At cubito-anal cross vein.
Ratio of anterior side of quadrangle to posterior side in front wing.	2:5	2:5	2:5	2:5	1:4
Same in hind wing.	2:3	2:3	2:3	2:3	1:2
Postquadrangular cells to level of intersection of R_s with M_{1-3} (antenodal cells).	3	3	3	3	3
Postnodals in front wing.	12 (2 wings).	11 (2 wings).	11 (2 wings). 12 (5 wings). 13 (1 wing).	11 (1 wing). 12 (3 wings). 13 (16 wings).	12 (1 wing). 13 (1 wing).
Same in hind wing.	11 (2 wings).	10 (2 wings).	11 (5 wings). 12 (3 wings).	10 (1 wing). 11 (3 wings). 12 (16 wings).	11 (2 wings).

Comparison of characters of species in the genus Metaleptobasis—Continued.

	bovilla, male.	*brysonima*, male.	*mauritia*, male.	*manicaria*, male.	*sp.*, female.
Origin of M_2 in front wing with reference to the postnodals.	Near 6th (2 wings).	Near 6th (1 wing). Between 5th and 6th (1 wing).	At 6th (2 wings). Near 7th (3 wings). At 7th (3 wings).	At 5th (3 wings). At 6th (13 wings). At 7th (4 wings).	At 6th (2 wings).
Same in hind wing.	Near 6th (2 wings).	At 5th (2 wings).	Near 6th (2 wings). At 6th (4 wings). Between 6th and 7th (1 wing). At 7th (1 wing).	At 5th (5 wings). At 6th (15 wings).	At 5th (2 wings).
Origin of M_{1a} in front wing with reference to the postnodals.	At 9th (2 wings).	At 8th (1 wing). At 9th (1 wing).	At 10th (2 wings). At 11th (6 wings).	At 9th (2 wings). At 10th (5 wings). At 11th (11 wings). At 12th (2 wings).	At 9th (2 wings).
Same in hind wing.	At 8th (2 wings).	At 9th (2 wings).	At 10th (5 wings). At 11th (2 wings). Between 11th and 12th (1 wing).	At 9th (4 wings). At 10th (8 wings). At 11th (8 wings).	At 8th (2 wings).
Cu_1 in front wing ending with reference to the postnodals.	At 8th (2 wings).	At 8th (2 wings).	At 9th (6 wings). At 10th (2 wings).	At 8th (2 wings). At 9th (6 wings). At 10th (12 wings).	At 8th (2 wings).
Same in hind wing.	At 8th (2 wings).	At 8th (2 wings).	At 8th (1 wing). At 9th (4 wings). At 10th (3 wings).	At 8th (2 wings). At 9th (9 wings). At 10th (9 wings).	At 8th (2 wings).
Cu_2 in front wing ending with reference to the postnodals.	At 5th (2 wings).	At 5th (2 wings).	At 6th (2 wings). At 7th (6 wings).	At 5th (2 wings). At 6th (3 wings). At 7th (11 wings). At 8th (4 wings).	At 3d (1 wing). At 4th (1 wing).
Same in hind wing.	At 5th (2 wings).	At 6th (2 wings).	At 6th (2 wings). At 7th (6 wings).	At 6th (2 wings). At 7th (15 wings). At 8th (3 wings).	At 4th (2 wings).

Brief mention may be made of earlier described species which are now referred to *Metaleptobasis*.

M. diceras was described by De Selys from a male with the last 4 segments lost and a female from Para. Calvert[1] refers a single male from Bahia, Brazil, to this species. No other specimens are known. Doctor Calvert figures the mesothoracic horns and the

[1] Calvert, Philip P. Contributions to a knowledge of the Odonata of the Neotropical Region, exclusive of Mexico and Central America, Ann. Carnegie Mus., vol. 6, No. 1, pp. 197-198, October 7, 1909.

abdominal appendages. If he is right in his determination, *diceras* can not be confused with any of the species I have before me because of the form of the appendages, which, in *diceras*, have the superiors large and robust in profile view, with the inferiors of apparently simple form and only about half as long as the superiors. De Selys describes *diceras* as having the mesothoracic horns slender and rather long. I am doubtful if this agrees well with Calvert's male. However, so far as the material before me goes, none of the species agrees with De Selys's description of the color of the head or the proportions of the anterior and posterior sides of the quadrangle.

M. bicornis was described by De Selys from a single female from the Amazon, has been recorded from Colombia by Brauer (1900), and described from an incomplete male, lacking the last 4 segments, by Calvert.[1] As Calvert points out, De Selys's description of the proportion of the anterior to the posterior side of the quadrangle in the front wing is undoubtedly a misprint, and should be 2:5, not 2:3. The color of the head of *bicornis* differs from any material before me. It is not impossible that the type female in De Selys's collection will prove unidentifiable through inability to associate it certainly with the proper male of any one of possibly two or more closely related species.

M. quadricornis was described by De Selys from a single female from Para. In this species there are nearly equal, rather short, conical horns on both the prothorax and mesothorax. The dorsum of the head is black.

M. cornicauda was described by Calvert[2] from a single male from Bahia, Brazil. It has no thoracic horns, and the superior appendages are robust, with the inferiors about one-third as long and of simple form. It is related to *macilenta*, according to Calvert, who regards *macilenta* as probably belonging to *Metaleptobasis*. *Macilenta* is known only from Rambur's type, a male in De Selys's collection.

2. TWO SPECIES OF PALAEMNEMA FROM GUATEMALA.

In material collected by myself in Guatemala in 1909 are 27 males[3] and 2 females of *Palaemnema paulina* (Drury), all taken at El Fiscal, Department Guatemala, June 3–6, except one male taken at Agua Caliente, a few miles below El Fiscal toward Puerto Barrios. (Agua Caliente of my itinerary of 1905 in Guatemala is a small village at some distance from the river; Agua Caliente, as now designated on the railroad from Puerto Barrios to Guatemala City, is a station, marked by a single building, situated on the right bank of the river, at the end of the railroad bridge, and possibly a mile distant from the

[1] Ann. Carnegie Mus., vol. 6, No. 1, 1909, p. 198.

[2] Idem, pp. 199–200.

[3] One of these males, collected on June 6, 1909, at El Fiscal, Department Guatemala, is in the United States National Museum collection.

little village, flanking the Government road over which we traveled by mule in 1905.) The collection also contains a male and female of *P. nathalia* Selys, taken at Gualan, Department Zacapa, the male on June 13, the female June 16, 1909. No Palaemnemas were taken by me in Guatemala in 1905, and the number of specimens known from other sources has been very limited. It was therefore deemed desirable to study this material carefully, with the view of determining the variability of certain characters, and especially to describe the female of *paulina* which has not hitherto been known.

I do not recall the circumstances under which the *P. nathalia* at Gualan were taken. I collected at widely separated localities on June 13 and 16, but there is no doubt, I think, that the male and female taken belong to the same species.

On the other hand I have a vivid recollection of the locality where *P. paulina* was found at El Fiscal. For some time prior to June 5, on which date there was a heavy rain in the afternoon at El Fiscal, there had been a continued and severe drought. Within a week after the first rain of June 5 the country had greened up beautifully. In the last stages of the drought all the water used by the Indian family with whom we lived at El Fiscal was carried from a small stream (called a river) flowing in a deep ravine about 1 mile or more north of the village. In places the sides of this ravine were perpendicular or even overhanging. Several times a large and extremely rapidly flying swift was seen here and parrots were often very numerous about holes in certain perpendicular dirt faces. At places the sides rose less abruptly and agaves were very numerous. At several points there were boggy spots on the sides of the ravine, about which grew some of the arums with other lush vegetation. *Hetaerina capitalis* was common in this ravine. The Palaemnemas occurred especially about the boggy spots, resting on larger leaved plants near the ground, and flying low and through brush to escape. One of the males, taken June 3, has a small fly in its mouth. The fly is a muscid, apparently one of the pomace flies.

In addition to the several characters mentioned below in which these two species differ, *nathalia* and *paulina* of both sexes may be at once separated by the form of the posterior ridge or keel of the occiput as seen in a direct dorsal view of the head. This ridge is equal in length to the distance between the antennæ, and directly posterior to each antenna is a distinct prominence on either end of this ridge or keel. In *paulina* the ridge is cut abruptly away externally at either end, leaving the prominence with a very distinct angle of about 90°; in *nathalia*, on the other hand, these prominences are low, symmetrical and rounded. I regret that I can not study this character in other species. It has not been mentioned in descriptions but its diagnostic value in the case of *paulina* and *nathalia* can not be overlooked.

In colors *nathalia* is a very much duller insect than *paulina*.

Comparison of characters of Palaemnema paulina and P. nathalia.

	paulina.	*nathalia.*
Labrum	Clear cream with lower half or third shining black, the colors sharply defined.	Bluish or greenish white with lower edge black, a dull violet indefinite band, equal in width to the pale basal area, between the pale area and the black edge.
Clypeus	Bluish or greenish white, postclypeus becoming dark with age and eventually black, at least in the male.	Dingy bluish white with the postclypeus, especially near the frons, tinged with violet.
Epicranium above the clypeus.	Shining black with bronze green reflections.	Shining black with bronze green reflections.
Prothorax	Colors sharply defined, the dark umber of dorsum of thorax continued on the posterior and median lobes and to a greater or less extent on the anterior lobe as a central spot, the blue (or yellow or greenish) pale antehumeral stripes carried straight across the posterior and median lobes on either side and spreading out over the anterior lobe.	Colors less sharply defined, both as regards contrast in colors themselves and in pattern. Pattern as described for *paulina*, but the dorsal color is a reddish brown and the lateral pale areas are flesh color with violet and dingy shadings.
Thorax	Dorsum dark rich umber; antehumeral stripe blue (or yellowish or greenish in younger individuals); sides blue with violet reflections, especially on the mesepimeron and metepimeron (in younger individuals and in two females these violet areas tend to deepen in color, while the other pale areas are yellowish); a dark stripe on the humeral and second lateral sutures, the latter the wider; mesinfraepisternum and propleuron dark.	Dorsum yellowish or greenish bronze, slightly less in extent than the dark dorsum of *paulina;* antehumeral stripes lilac; sides about as in *paulina*, so far as the limited material goes; mesinfraepisternum dark, but propleuron pale, not dark as in *paulina*.
Legs	Coxae all pale; legs flesh color; femora dark to black superiorly; first tibiae darker than the others, especially inferiorly.	Similar to *paulina*, but all tibiae the same color, and slightly darker than the last two pairs in *paulina*.
Abdomen	Male dorsum of 1 and 2 black, widest apically; 3-7 with basal cream-colored rings interrupted middorsally on 3; 8 and 9 lilac; 10 black; female similar to the male except last 3 segments; 8 is entirely black, 9 has a large irregular dorsal spot pale dingy yellowish, this spot narrowly separated from the base of the segment in the middorsal line, separated from the apex by its own width, on the sides of the segment produced apically, and separated from the apex by only a narrow margin, widely separated from the lower margin of the segment; 10 and appendages dark; apex of ovipositor clear pale yellow.	Male similar to *paulina*, basal rings on 3-7 narrower, duller and less produced apically along the lower lateral margin of each segment; 10 apparently with some of the dorsum pale colored; female similar to *paulina* but the spot on 9 is less sharply defined and is slightly larger.
Length of abdomen (mm.).	Male, 37.5-43.5; average of 10, 39.95; female, 34-35.5.	Male, 32.5; female, 30.
Length of hind wing (mm.).	Male, 27-32; average of 10, 29.45; female, 27-29.	Male and female, 24.5.
Postnodals, front wing.	Male, 21-28 (3 wings have 21; 2, 22; 2, 23; 7, 24; 2, 25; 3, 26; 1, 28), average of 20 wings, 23.85; female, 22-24 (1 wing has 22; 1, 23; 2, 24).	Male, 22-23; female, 22.
Postnodals, hind wing.	Male, 18-23 (2 wings have 18; 3, 19; 3, 20; 7, 21; 3, 22; 2, 23), average of 20 wings, 20.6; female, 20-21 (2 wings have 20; 2, 21).	Male, 19; female, 20-21.

Comparison of characters of Palaemnema paulina and P. nathalia—Continued.

	paulina.	*nathalia.*
Cu_1 ending beyond origin of M_{1a} in front wing (i. e., number of marginal cells posterior to Cu_1 apical to origin of M_{1a}).	Male, 2–9 cells (1 wing has 2; 1, 3; 1, 3.5; 1, 4; 2, 5; 1, 5.5; 1, 6; 5, 7; 1, 7.5; 4, 8; 2, 9), average of 20 wings, 6.32; female, 3–6 (1 wing has 3; 1, 3.5; 2, 6).	Male, 5 and 7; female, 4.5 and 6.5.
Same of hind wing.	Male, 7–13 cells (2 wings have 7; 1, 7.5; 1, 8; 1, 8.5; 3, 9; 1, 9.5; 2, 10; 3, 11; 1, 11.5; 4, 12; 1, 13), average of 20 wings, 10; female, 7.5–10 (1 wing has 7.5; 1, 8; 1, 9; 1, 10).	Male, 11 and 13; female, 9.
Number of cells surmounted by stigma, front wing.	Male, 2–3.5 (5 wings 2; 9, 2.5; 5, 3; 1, 3.5), average of 20 wings, 2.55; female, 2–3 (1 wing 2; 2, 2.5; 1, 3).	Male and female, 2.
Same of hind wing..	Male, 2–3 (1 wing 2; 9, 2.5; 10, 3), average of 20 wings, 2.725; female, 2.	Male, 2; female, 1.5 and 2.

In two front wings and one hind wing of the 10 males of *paulina* carefully studied the cubito-anal cross-vein is midway or slightly closer to the first antenodal; in all the others it is closer to the second antenodal. The unusual condition is due to the more apical position of the first antenodal in these cases, the position of the second antenodal being relatively fixed by its relation to the arculus (some slight variation, as the second antenodal is at or slightly proximal to the arculus). When the second antenodal is proximal to the arculus the result is that the cubito-anal cross-vein is placed relatively nearer the second antenodal. To sum up, variation in this character—the cubito-anal cross-vein nearer the first or second antenodal—might arise from 3 widely different causes: (1) The subquadrangle may be lengthened basally, and the cubito-anal cross-vein may really be placed basally with reference to other wing structures; or (2) the first antenodal may be moved apically or basally, shortening or lengthening the distance between the antenodals; or (3) the second antenodal may be moved apically or basally, lengthening or shortening the distance between the antenodals. Of course one or all of these conditions might be present in the same wing.

All the specimens of *Palaemnema* in my collection have been examined as to the number of antenodals. Variation is shown in this character in 3 front wings and 1 hind wing of males of *paulina*, in each of which there are 3 antenodals in the first series. Two of the front wings belong to the same individual; the other 2 cases are in two individuals. In the case of the 3 front wings the added antenodal is basal to the normal antenodals; in the hind wing it is placed between the 2 normal antenodals. The variation differs therefore from the condition found normally in *Thaumatoneura* and several calopterygine genera with reduced venation in which the added number of antenodals confined to the first series are apical to the specialized and strengthened 2 continuous antenodals.

Normally the 4-sided subquadrangle is joined by a single short cross-vein (part of A) to the posterior wing margin, but in all the material before me 1 front wing and 2 hind wings of males of *paulina* have this area 5-sided, with 2 short cross-veins to the posterior wing margin. One front wing and 1 hind wing showing this character were the left wings of 1 individual.

The apices of the wings of all the females and of the male of *nathalia* are without trace of dark color. Wings of both sexes except very teneral individuals and the male of *nathalia* show more or less whitish opalescence, especially on the hind wings and especially beyond the nodus. Since the female of *nathalia* shows this opalescence it may be expected in the male, but the single specimen I have shows only a narrow margin of it about the stigma.

The apical brown on the wings of males of *paulina* is ontogenetic; teneral males show no trace of it, and in the most mature specimens I have it is most extensive and darkest in color. My material is largely teneral, and the following data relating to the 27 males indicate this:

Apices of wings without trace of dark color, 13 individuals.
Apices of wings beyond stigma slightly fumose, 6 individuals.
Apices of wings beyond stigma fumose, 4 individuals.
Apices of wings beyond middle of stigma fumose, 3 individuals.
Apices of wings from level of stigma black, 1 individual.

In view of the ontogenetic character of this wing marking it remains to be seen if *angelina*, as determined by Doctor Calvert,[1] is distinct from *paulina*.

Male abdominal appendages.—In the entire series of *paulina* examined there seems to be no noteworthy variation. The superior appendage on its ventro-internal edge is squarely narrowed, at a distance from the apex less than the width of the appendage at this point, for slightly more than half the width of the appendage, the supero-external edge opposite this cut-out being convex and continuous to the apex. The outline shown in most dorsal views differs from Doctor Calvert's[2] figure 40, therefore, in that the inner subapical emargination is more marked, the inclosed angle being nearly a right angle, rather than a very obtuse angle. In addition to the spine on the supero-external edge of the superiors, as shown in Doctor Calvert's figure, there is on the same edge a similar smaller spine, placed slightly closer to the apex than to the basal spine, the edge between the spines being concave. The basal spine is not quite so heavy as

[1] Biologia Centrali-Americana, Odonata, p. 136, February, 1903.
[2] Idem, pl. 5.

shown in Doctor Calvert's figure. Viewed in profile the inferior appendage at about its middle on the ventral edge has a distinct prominence, this prominence being opposite the origin of the basal tooth shown on the inner edge of the inferior appendage in Doctor Calvert's figure. In my material this tooth and the area supporting it extending along the inner side of the appendage to its base is pale colored and apparently less chitinized than the remaining basal portions of the appendage. The apex of the lower appendage terminates in a very narrow, suddenly constricted, flattened, thread-like body, shining and horn like, which resembles a claw or hook on the appendage, curved in directly toward the appendage in a semicircle opposed to the curve of the appendage itself. The tip of this small thread-like body is rounded. Opposed to this curved thread-like end of the appendage and opposite its tip is a minute spine on the appendage. This thread-like body is not discernible on all specimens because of the position of the appendages in drying and because of its small size and optical indistinctness. In life it is probably flexible and, in connection with the spine opposite it, is intimately concerned with the coupling of the sexes.

In the single male of *nathalia* the second spine described above on the supero-external edge of the superiors is minute or wanting and the edge is not concave as in *paulina*. The lower edge of the inferiors, seen in profile, is convex at about the middle but has no distinct prominence as has *paulina*. I detect a similar thread-like apical termination as in that species, but the position of the appendages makes it impossible to study this carefully, and I can not see any minute opposing spine as described for *paulina*.

3. A NEW TELAGRION FROM TRINIDAD, WITH A NOTE ON TELAGRION DAECKII BY PHILIP P. CALVERT.

The following is a brief description of a new *Telagrion* collected by Mr. B. J. Rainey in Trinidad.

TELAGRION RAINEYI, new species.

Male.—Length of abdomen, 31 mm.; length of hind wing, 17.5.

Labium pale yellowish, median lobe with a U-shaped cleft for about two-fifths its length. Labrum dark green, very narrowly margined with pale yellow. Clypeus and dorsum of head black, marked as follows: A median yellow spot and on either side a smaller spot between clypeus and frons; occiput, on either side of the occipital ridge behind the ocelli, dull orange, separated from the eyes by a black line; through this orange is a dull black band, about one-third as wide as the orange at the eyes, and extending from the occipital ridge to the eyes, nearly parallel to the rear of the head; overlying the outer end of this black band and the yellow adjacent to it anteriorly are blue postocular spots. The occipital yellow inclosed between the vertex, the black band above described, and the eye appears as a triangular yellow spot on either side; the apex of the triangle is opposite and separated from the lateral ocellus, and the base of the triangle is parallel to the eye, from which it is narrowly separated by black. That these yellow spots are in reality a part of the larger occipital yellow area, traversed by the black band above described, is evident only after careful examination. On the rear of the head below this yellow occipital area is a transverse broken black line, below which

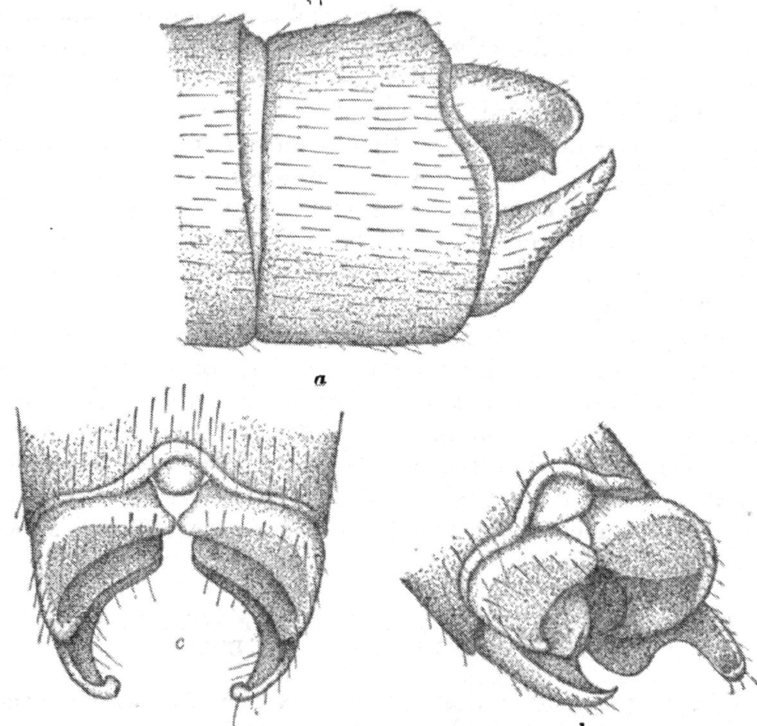

LATERAL, DORSAL, AND OBLIQUE VIEWS OF THE MALE APPENDAGES OF *Telagrion raineyi*.

the rear of the head is pale yellowish. Gena above the labrum-clypeus suture black, below pale yellowish. First joint of antenna black, about two-thirds length of the second joint, which is light brown, dark brown at apex. Eyes dull green, brown above, paler below.

Thorax below pale yellow. Prothorax dark green above, posterior lobe laterally pale yellow, hind border low, rounded, entire. Mesepisternum brownish green; overlying this ground color on either side a bright pale blue antehumeral stripe, this stripe about one-third the width of the mesepisternum, of uniform width, and straight. Mesepimeron golden and green indefinitely. Metepisternum blue, paler than the antehumeral stripe, and with pale yellowish and greenish showing through. Metepimeron flesh colored, its posterior and lower fourth (a triangular area) bright yellow as though overlaid with pigment, traces of green showing in the yellow. Coxae and legs pale yellow, spines short and sparse, dark brown; tarsal claws light brown, darker at apex, a minute tooth present.

Abdominal segment 1 brown above in median line, sides above greenish blue, basally and below light yellow; 2 brown above, darker apically, sides above greenish blue, below light yellow; 3–8 black above, 3–5 with greenish reflections, brightest on 3 and successively duller on following segments; interrupted basal rings on 3–7, narrower and complete on 8, greenish blue on 3, pale yellowish on 4–8; 3–7 greenish yellow beneath, brighter on the proximal segments, becoming duller, darker and obscured on the distal segments; dorsal color carried on the sides apically of 3–6 as lateral spots; sides of 7 largely and of 8 entirely dark; 9–10 bright light blue; superior appendages brown, inferiors pale flesh.

Stigma very dark brown, sides subequal, oblique, covering less than one cell. Quadrangle of front wing with ratio of anterior to posterior side 2:5; of hind wing 2:3. Postnodals, front wings 10, hind wings 8 or 9. Arculus at second antenodal. Posterior wing margin meeting A slightly distal to cubito-anal cross-vein in front wing, and at the cubito-anal cross-vein in hind wing. R_s arising from the vein of the nodus; M_3 in front wing arising from almost the same point, in the hind wing very closely to the vein of the nodus but appreciably proximal to it; in all four wings R_s and M_3 closely approximated at the first cross-vein between them and widely separated from M_4 at the same point. M_2 in front wing arising just proximal to fifth postnodal, in hind wing just proximal to fourth postnodal. M_{1a} arising in front wing at eighth postnodal, in hind wing at seventh or eighth. Cu_1 in front wing terminating on a level between fifth and sixth postnodals or at the sixth, in the hind wing at about the sixth; Cu_2 in front and hind wings terminating at the third postnodal.

Described from a single male in my collection taken March 10, 1912, at a small swamp near Cumuto, Trinidad, described on page 601 of this paper, by Mr. B. J. Rainey, to whom I am indebted for this and many more dragonflies, and for whom I take pleasure in naming the species.

The following brief notes on colors made from the freshly killed insect will give some idea of its peculiar beauty when alive. Dorsum of thorax black, a vivid ultramarine blue line just above the humeral suture. Below this blue line and all of the mesepimeron dark dull green; metepisternum largely vivid emerald; metepimeron pale lemon yellow. Eyes beneath emerald, above nile green; vivid ultramarine irregularly rounded postocular spots. Legs pale yellow, translucent. Abdomen: apex of 1, all of 2 and base of 3 laterally vivid blue as on thorax and postocular spots; sides of 3–7 yellowish;

dorsum of 3–8 black, little if any metallic; 9–10 bright sky blue, unmarked.

My reasons for referring this insect to *Telagrion* are the same as stated by Calvert in describing his *T. daeckii*,[1] in which paper the venation of both *T. daeckii* and *T. longum* Selys is figured. The blue postocular spots of *raineyi* are likely to prove evanescent in dried material. From the described species of *Telagrion*, *raineyi* is distinct by many characters. *T. fulvellum* Selys and *T. inversum* Selys have the abdomen reddish, and in these 2 species and in *longum* the last 3 segments are red or reddish yellow. *T. mecistogastrum* Selys is a larger dragonfly, with the abdomen of the male 50–52 mm. in length. *T. daeckii* has the apex of 7 and 8–10 pale blue.

The following notes on *Telagrion daeckii* by Dr. Philip P. Calvert have been added to this paper at my request:

TELAGRION DAECKII Calvert.

The recently killed male shows the following colors when compared with the original description:[2] Eyes blue above, becoming pale greenish below; the blue of the head, except the labrum, is mixed with greenish and hence not so pure as that of labrum, thorax, and abdomen; prothorax with a transverse line near the hind dorsal margin; mid-dorsal thoracic carina narrowly blue, dividing the median black stripe longitudinally; metallic green on abdominal segment 7 ending posteriorly in three prolongations, one mid-dorsal, the other two wider and infero-lateral.

In the recently killed female the eyes are pale olive above to pale green below, with two horizontal blackish stripes running from anterior to posterior margin of the eye, the upper stripe at about one-fifth, the lower at two-fifths the eye-height from the upper surface; these stripes sub-equal in width to the pale color which separates them. Heads generally paler and a little more greenish than in the male, this especially true of the labrum. Thorax pale olive green, with black markings as in the male, almost white on the sides inferiorly. Dorsum of abdominal segments 1–8 dark metallic green, widened just in front of the hind end of 2–6 and almost interrupted at the base of 3–7; sides of 1–6 pale green, of 7 and 8 and all of 9 and 10 (except a transverse dorsal basal black stripe or line on 9) pale blue, paler than the same segments of the male.

Appendages one-third as long as 10, pale bluish. Genital valves not reaching farther than the level of the middle of 10, their "palpi" barely extending beyond the level of the hind margin of 10. A stout vulvar spine on the hind ventral end of the sternum of 8. Hind margin of prothorax shaped almost as in the male, perhaps a trifle more produced dorsad.

Abdomen, 32.5–31.5 mm.; hind wing, 21.

Pairs of this species were seen flying together, the male clasping the female with his appendages, the bodies of the two forming an almost continuously straight line, moving rather slowly and stately among the *Pontederia* and *Nymphaea* (*Castalia*) near the banks of the mill pond at Malaga, New Jersey, June 27 and July 2, 1913.

4. SOME STUDIES OF PROTONEURA.

In 1860 De Selys brought under his new *sous-genre Protoneura* 3 species—*capillaris*, *tenuis*, and *sancta*. The first considered and best known, *capillaris* Rambur, must be regarded as the type of the

[1] Ent. News, vol. 14, p. 38, February, 1903.

[2] Idem, p. 36, February, 1903.

genus. In 1886, in his Revision du Synopsis des Agrionines, the American agrionines lacking Cu_2 were considered a *genre Protoneura,* 2 subgenera, *Microneura* (with long legs with long and numerous bristles) and *Protoneura* (with short legs and moderate, less numerous bristles) being recognized. Under this last, 10 species are described, and a careful grouping of the species, based on venational characters, is worked out. These groupings serve admirably as an aid in the identification of species, but, as might be expected, larger material shows that in a very few details they are artificial. For example, the very different wings, figures 4 and 7 of plates 41 and 42, would fall together; and figure 10, plate 42, combines characters in such a way as to exclude it from both of De Selys's groups.

Doctor Calvert[1] describes (or redescribes) 6 new species, bringing the Central American species up to 7, for which 7 species groupings similar to De Selys's, but amplified by other venational and other than venational characters, are given. This summary covers briefly about all that has been written on the relationships within the genus of the 16 known species.

The study of British Guiana material collected by B. J. Rainey and L. A. and E. B. Williamson led to a study of the groupings within the genus in relation both to the known species and to new species in this material. The conclusion has been that groups of generic rank are recognizable, and that it is desirable at this time to separate *Protoneura* into 4 genera. Venational differences between closely related agrionine genera are much more marked in the legion *Protoneura* than in the legion *Agrion,* for example. In the present paper *calverti, corculum,* and *amatoria* (see figs. 1, 2, and 3, pl. 41), for example, are considered congeneric, though they differ in two striking venational characters—the proportions of the 3 antenodal costal spaces,[2] and the ending of Cu_1. In the characters of Cu_1 *corculum* is like *calverti;* in its antenodal costal spaces it is like *amatoria.* If *calverti* and *amatoria* were separated generically the question of the generic position of *corculum* would be in doubt, and two decisions, in the absence of other determining factors, would be possible: One of the two characters could be regarded as the more important and *corculum* could be associated generically with one or the other species; or a new genus could be erected for *corculum.* That is to say, with our present knowledge, the existence of the species *corculum,* having one venational character of *calverti* and another venational character of *amatoria,* makes the generic separation of *calverti* and *amatoria* impractical. Were the number of

[1] Biologia Centrali-Americana, Neuroptera, pp. 140–145, April, 1903, and 394–397, Nov., 1907.

[2] The first antenodal costal space is the space from the wing base to the first antenodal; the second antenodal costal space is the space between the antenodals; and the third antenodal costal space is the space from the second antenodal to the nodus.

species involved large, and were such possible new genera not monotypic, added convenience might permit the erection of such new genera; at the present time there seems no warrant for such a minute breaking up of the genus.

The four genera recognized in the present study are described in the following key and tabulation of venational characters. They are as follows:

1. *Protoneura;* type, *capillaris* Rambur.
2. *Epipleoneura*, new genus; type, *lamina*, new species.
3. *Psaironeura*, new genus; type, *remissa* Calvert.
4. *Epipotoneura*, new genus; type, *nehalennia*, new species.

The new generic names are suggestive of the manner of flight of these insects. In their compounding and in the selection of specific names for the six new species described in this paper I have had the advice of Prof. J. B. Parker.

In agrionine wings generally, and in those with reduced venation especially, any shifting of one of the larger veins results in other striking readjustments of other parts. Consequently in such wings as *Protoneura calverti*, for example, where the maximum reduction of American agrionines is reached, there is a relative fixity of parts, which in a more complex wing might shift position with but little effect on adjoining parts. For example, the postnodals generally have well-defined descending cross veins with one of which M_2 bears a definite relation.[1] The origin of M_2 is thus, when once fixed, pretty rigidly held in its place. When one part or character of a wing is located or described by reference to another part, and variation appears, it may be impossible or difficult to tell which part has shifted. For example, variation in the position of the cubito-anal cross vein relative to the first antenodal may result from the shifting of either one or both of the two veins. A series of wing photographs of a species, enlarged to the same scale, would enable one to determine the definiteness or instability of the position in the wing of the cubito-anal cross vein, the antenodals, the arculus, the nodus, and other parts. Such a study should be made in the interests of accuracy in defining the position of these parts. In tabulating wings I have noticed some shifting of the cubito-anal cross vein and both antenodals, and have detected no instability in the arculus or nodus. In one species it was noticed that, when the second antenodal is close to the arculus, the upper limb of the arculus is shorter than when the antenodal is more proximal.

[1] Compare the definite and normal bracing of these parts in *calverti* (fig. 1), for example, with the weak and unusual arrangement shown in the front wing of *remissa* (fig. 9), pls. 41 and 42.

KEY TO THE GENERA AND SPECIES.

a^1. Wings narrow, width about one-seventh the length or less; first antenodal costal space longer than the third, and about twice or more the second; R_s arising at the subnodus, M_3 proximal; M_2 arising at or just proximal to the fifth postnodal in the front wings, at or just proximal to the fourth in the hind wings; M_3 ending distal to the stigma.. *Protoneura*.[1]

b^1. Cu_1 ending against or at the termination of the cross vein descending from the subnodus.[2]

c^1. Wings extremely narrow, the width about one-eighth the length; base to nodus over one-third the wing length and equaling the distance from the nodus to beyond the sixth postnodal; first antenodal costal space nearly equaling the other two.. *calverti*.

c^2. Wing width about one-seventh the length; base to nodus about one-third the wing length and equaling the distance from the nodus to beyond the fifth postnodal; first antenodal costal space only slightly longer than the third.. *corculum*.

b^2. Cu_1 produced beyond the cross vein descending from the subnodus; otherwise like *corculum* above.[3] The Central American species may be separated as follows:

c^1. Inferior appendages of the male as seen in profile with an acute superior tooth, or the inferiors longer than the superiors; dorsum of thorax of female predominantly black, or mesostigmal spine wanting.

d^1. Male and female thoracic dorsum predominantly black; female with mesostigmal spine present.

e^1. Abdominal segments 3–7 of male with small dorsal basal blue spots; female not separable from the next species.......................... *cupida*.

e^2. Dorsum of abdominal segments 3–7 of male basally three-fourths or more red; female not separable from the preceding species........ *amatoria*.

d^2. Male and female thoracic dorsum predominantly orange; dorsum of abdominal segment 3 of male with basal half or more yellow, 4–7 with very narrow basal rings (or wanting on 5–7); female without mesostigmal spine.. *aurantiaca*.

c^2. Inferior appendages of the male without an acute superior tooth, abdominal segments 3–7 with deep yellow narrow basal rings; female without mesostigmal spine.. *cara*.

---

[1] *Protoneura peramans* Calvert from Guatemala is known to me only from descriptions and I am not certain of its generic position. Specifically it may be recognized at once by the following characters: Abdomen, male 42–43 mm., female 36–37 mm.; hind wing, male 23–24 mm., female 25.5–27 mm.; R_s arising at the subnodus, M_3 proximal; Cu_1 produced beyond the cross vein descending from the subnodus; M_2 arising nearest the sixth or seventh postnodal in the front wings, nearest the fifth in the hind wings.

[2] *P. paucinervis* Selys and *P. exigua* Selys probably belong here, but are known to me only from descriptions which do not enable me to determine their relationships to *calverti* and *corculum*. Some specific characters of the 4 species are discussed under *calverti*.

[3] Four South American species may belong under b^2 under a^1, or more probably they belong in *Epipleoneura* under b^1 under a^2. The 4 species may be briefly discussed:

ephippigera Selys.—Male. Thorax above and laterally, excepting the metepimeron, shining black; abdomen 35–37 mm., hind wing 20–22 mm.; female not known; South America.

humeralis Selys.—Female only known; considered by De Selys as possibly the female of *ephippigera*; mesepisternum and mesepimeron black with a yellow humeral line; posterior border of prothorax with a V-shaped excavation; abdomen 28 mm., hind wing 20 mm.; South America.

tenuis Selys.—Not well described and known only from De Selys's notes on 3 specimens from the Amazon. The original description (1860) and the later note (1886) have little in common; abdomen 26 mm., hind wing 16 mm.

capilliformis Selys.—Male. Mesepisternum and mesepimeron black, with a fine, obscure, incomplete line on the middorsal carina; abdomen 27 mm., hind wing 16 mm.; female not described, though, to De Selys's original Brazilian record, Calvert adds 3 males, 1 female (Odonata of the Neotropical Region, Ann. Carnegie Mus., p. 212).

a^2. Wings not so narrow, the width one-sixth the length or more; first and third antenodal costal spaces about equal, the first less than twice the second; distance from base to nodus one-third the wing length or slightly less.

b^1. R_s arising at the subnodus, M_3 proximal; Cu_1 produced beyond the cross vein descending from the subnodus .... *Epipleoneura*.[1]

c^1. M_2 arising at the third postnodal in the hind wings.

d^1. M_2 arising at the fourth postnodal in the front wings; the second antenodal costal space shorter than the other two .... *incusa*.

d^2. M_2 arising at the fifth or distal to the fourth postnodal in the front wings, the 3 antenodal costal spaces subequal .... *fuscaenea*,

c^2. M_2 arising midway between the third and fourth or proximal to the fourth postnodal in the hind wings, at the fifth or more distal in the front wings, the second antenodal costal space shorter than the other two....... *lamina*.

b^2. R_s arising distal to the subnodus, M_3 proximal, at or distal to the subnodus, or R_s and M_3 joined at their origin into a single vein arising at or distal to the subnodus.

c^1. Cu_1 ending at the cross vein descending from the subnodus, the three antenodal costal spaces about equal .... *Psaironeura*.

d^1. Dorsum of thorax and last abdominal segments with much red or yellow.

e^1. Superior appendages of the male subcylindrical, the inferiors terminated by a small, blunt, curved point .... *tenuissima*.[2]

e^2. Superior appendages of the male forked, the inferiors without a point. *cerasina*.

d^2. Dorsum of the thorax and last abdominal segments with little or no red or yellow.

e^1. Abdomen of female 31 mm., 8 and 9 black; hind wing 19–20 mm .. *remissa*.

e^2. Abdomen of female 26 mm., 8 and 9 with basal articulations and the apex of 9 pale; hind wing 19 mm................................ *sancta*.[3]

c^2. Cu_1 produced beyond the cross vein descending from the subnodus; M_2 arising at the fifth postnodal in the front wings, at the third or proximal to the fourth in the hind wings; first and third antenodal costal spaces about equal, the second much shorter, but more than one-half the third; stigma long and narrow, more than twice as long as wide. *Epipotoneura nehalennia*.

The discussion of various species collected follows.

PROTONEURA CALVERTI, new species.

Length of abdomen, male 32–34 mm., female 27–29; hind wing, male 17.5–18.5 mm., female 18–19.

Head.—Male. Shining black; labium pale flesh colored; genae bright yellow; 4 duller yellow spots across the head, 1 at the base of each antenna, and 2 on the frons in front; rear of head black.

Female. Black; dorsum with metallic green and violet reflections; labium pale flesh; genae almost white, greenish tinged; anteclypeus with 3 pale spots, obscure or wanting; 4 spots across the head as in the male, but larger and clear pale yellow.

---

[1] See note 3 on p. 619.

[2] *Tenuissima* Selys from the Amazon is known to me only from description; both sexes are known. In coloration it is scarcely distinguishable from *cerasina*.

[3] Only the female of *sancta* Hagen from Brazil is known, and this to me only from descriptions.

Prothorax.—Male. Black; a large orange (red in life) spot on the middle lobe, slightly narrower at the middle and divided by the merest line of black; hind lobe slightly emarginate at the center.

Female. Black; a light yellow spot on the side of each lobe, forming an interrupted lateral stripe, which is continued onto the mesothorax by a spot on the mesothoracic lamina; hind lobe convex.

Thorax.—Male. Black; mesepisternum with a large triangular orange (red in life) spot below; this spot is about half the length of the mesepisternum and below attains nearly the full width of the mesepisternum, reaching the humeral suture and separated from its fellow on the opposite side narrowly by black in the middorsal line; the black inclosed between the orange spots is triangular in shape, the apex below; an isolated, short and wide band of pale bluish on the metepisternum, surrounding the metastigma; metepimeron pale bluish below for its entire length, the pale encroaching most on the black near the middle of the second lateral suture, which however is not reached by the pale area; metasternum pale flesh, a black transverse band just posterior to the third coxae.

Female. Black; middorsal carina and a narrow humeral stripe pale yellow, the latter more or less interrupted above at one or two points; metepisternum with a flesh colored or pale yellow area similar to the same area in the male but more extensive; below similar to the male. No mesostigmal spines or processes.

Abdomen.—Male. Black; 1 and 2 each with a lateral, quadrate, pale blue spot; ventral edge of sides of segments 7–9 yellowish, wider on 8, very narrow on the other two; 3–6 very long and slender, 4–6 each slightly longer than 3; these 4 segments make up over three-fourths the total length of the abdomen. Appendages black, the superiors brown at the middle.

Female. Black; 1–2 similar to the male; very narrow basal rings on 3–6; a narrow ventral edge of yellowish on sides of 6–9, wider on 8 and 9. Genital valves slightly exceeding 10, the long slender palps slightly exceeding the conical black appendages, which are shorter than 10.

Legs.—Male. Coxae and the extreme base of femora flesh colored; otherwise all black.

Female similar to the male, but basal half (first legs) to two-thirds (last legs) of the femora pale, the pale area with a median brown patch.

Wings clear and shining; stigma black in the male, dark brown in the female. The 3 antenodal costal spaces of the front wing of a male are in length, respectively, 6, 3, 3½ in units of an eyepiece micrometer; of a hind wing, 5¾, 3, 3. In the front wing the total, 12½, reaches from the nodus almost to the eighth postnodal; in the hind wing the total, 11¾, reaches to just beyond the seventh postnodal. In the front wing of a female the spaces measure 5, 2⅔, 3⅔;

the total, 11⅓, reaching from the nodus to just proximal to the seventh postnodal. The spaces of the hind wing measure 5, 2⅓, 3½; the total, 10⅚, reaching from the nodus to just distal to the sixth postnodal. In the 25 wings of this species tabulated as to various characters, the stalks of the sectors of the arculus were studied but not tabulated. In 2 front wings and 2 hind wings only short stalks were present, but in all other cases the stalk of the sectors was long or very long—the longest detected in all the wings of the various species tabulated. It is possible that this character should have been added to those tabulated.

Described from 16 males and 6 females, Cashew Creek, Tumatumari, British Guiana, February 8, 9, and 11, 1912, and 4 males, 1 female, small creek just above Potaro Landing, British Guiana, February 10, 1912. Type, a male, and allotype, a female from Tumatumari, February 8, in my collection. Named for Dr. Philip P. Calvert, whose leadership in systematic American Odonatology for 20 years has won the gratitude and admiration of all students of dragonflies.

Paratypes.—Cat. No. 19214, U.S.N.M. A male and a female from Tumatumari, British Guiana, February 9, 1912.

Cashew Creek is a small sluggish stream, during low-water stage 2 to 6 feet wide, flowing in a mud bed through woods. During low-water stage it is the first flowing water entering Potaro River above Tumatumari on the same side of the river. Just above Potaro Landing is a similar smaller and more shaded stream. In shade this species is all but invisible on the wing. As the males came out in the sunlight, to flutter almost motionless near the water's surface, the red thoracic spots would suddenly appear like tiny flames to attract the attention of the collector. Usually some time elapsed before the rest of the insect could be discerned and its position determined. When they moved the direction of flight could rarely be seen. After some experience with them I became more adept in locating them over the water and could more quickly distinguish the various parts of the body. But a hurried collector, and one unappreciative of the phantomlike character of some of the slender, shade-frequenting tropical agrionines, might have passed up and down the creek many times without detecting the presence of this beautiful and graceful insect. Twice in Trinidad at different small streams I caught the flame-flash of the red-spotted thorax of this or a similar species, but in neither case was I able to obtain a second glimpse of the insect itself.

The female oviposits in submerged leaves, the apex of the abdomen brought almost directly beneath the wing bases, the first 4 segments held aloft and the last 6 segments directed almost vertically downward, in a position suggestive of an ovipositing ichneumon-fly, *Thalessa*.

Of the four species, *paucinervis* Selys, *exigua* Selys, *corculum* Calvert, and *calverti*, both sexes are known. The first two species, from Brazil, are known to me only from descriptions. *Paucinervis* is, to judge by color, closely related to *corculum*, but it remains to be seen whether its venational characters are those of *corculum* or *calverti*. Venationally the same is to be said of *exigua*, in which the thoracic pattern (little black and similar in the two sexes) and the shorter inferior appendages of the male suggest an altogether different relationship. Specifically the 4 may be separated as follows:

Male.—Dorsum of thorax largely black, with large, isolated, trangular red spots on lower half..*calverti*.
Dorsum of thorax largely yellow or red.
This red or yellow isolated on dorsum..........................*corculum*.
This red or yellow continuous with pale lateral areas.
Mesepimeron with black..............................*paucinervis*.
Mesepimeron without black..................................*exigua*.
Female.—Thorax largely orange..*exigua*.
Dorsum of thorax largely black.
Metepimeron with black markings..............................*calverti*.
Metepimeron without black.
Metepisternum with some black above..................*corculum*.
Metepisternum without black above.................*paucinervis*.

PROTONEURA CORCULUM Calvert.

Morales, Guatemala, May 27, 1909, 3 males. This is the second record for this species, the original material, 2 males, 1 female, having been taken at Livingston, Guatemala. The pale dorsal thoracic color is red, not pale blue as described. For a discussion of relationships, see under *P. calverti*.

PROTONEURA AMATORIA Calvert.

Morales, Guatemala, May 27, 1909, 1 male; Los Amates, June 21, 1909, 5 males, 2 females.

Costa Rica: Rio Tizate, south of Turrucares, December 22 and 23, 1909, Calvert and Tristan, 21 males. A pair of the specimens from Los Amates is deposited in the United States National Museum.

Trinidad: Diegomartin River, near Port of Spain, February 29, 1912, 2 males, 1 female. Diegomartin is a small stream, at low-water stage with much of its bed dry. Like other hill streams about Port of Spain, it is very easy to follow the stream's bed, as the water is generally shallow and the bottom hard. Clumps of bamboo grow on the immediate banks at many places along Diegomartin, and below the mass of tough fibrous roots which form a vertical bank are frequently pools of deeper water. *Amatoria* was taken in the shadow of these masses of bamboo roots. Its capture in Trinidad, far from where I collected the types in Honduras, was indeed a surprise.

Doctor Calvert has made the following notes on living Costa Rica material:

Male: Eyes bright red in uppermost third, brown in middle third, pale green in lowermost third, these three colors marked off distinctly from one another in horizontal bands; one black pseudopupilla visible in each band, but less distinctly in the brown. Body colors red, black, and yellow, the last as a transverse median line on frons, a narrow margin to the free edge of the labrum, genae, labium, most of metapleura, pectus, legs, sides, and ventral surface of segment 1, and ventral edges of tergites of 2–9. Female: Eyes colored as in the male but the red less bright and less extensive; no red on the rest of the body, which is dark brown (thorax) and black (abdomen), marked with yellow. This species flew along the banks, close to the water, where it was shallow and not very swift. The male and female flew together, the male holding the female, which oviposited in submerged leaves fallen from the trees overhead.

The variation in the extent of red on the mesepisternum of the male is very great and is apparently independent of locality, Doctor Calvert's material from one locality in Costa Rica showing all variations. In the darkest phase the antehumeral red area at its widest point is less than half as wide as the black area lying between it and the middorsal carina, and is separated from the antealar red spots by a distance about equal to the width of the mesepisternum. Three of Doctor Calvert's 21 males show this pattern. Thirteen males are about the pattern shown in figure 15 (pl. 43.) Five have the antehumeral and antealar red joined, in two cases the red constricted at the point of joining, while in the remaining three this point is entirely obliterated, the broad red antehumeral stripe extending from the wings to and onto the prothorax, completely isolating the oval-shaped middorsal black, which, on either side of the middorsal carina, occupies an area on the mesepisternum about equal to the red. The specimens from Trinidad are colored like the 13 Costa Rica males.

PROTONEURA CUPIDA Calvert.

Los Amates, Guatemala, June 19, 1909, 1 male, along Rio San Francisco, a small stream 10 to 20 feet wide.

PROTONEURA CARA Calvert.

Agua Caliente, Department of Santa Rosa, Guatemala, June 2, 1909, 2 teneral males; Gualan, Guatemala, June 14, 1909, 1 male.

PROTONEURA AURANTIACA Selys.

Los Amates, Guatemala, June 21, 1909, 5 males, 1 female, along a small wet-weather stream in woods. One of the male specimens is deposited in the United States National Museum.

Some doubt existed as to the identification of *aurantiaca*,[1] so a male was sent to Monsieur Severin for comparison with the De Selys material. Doctor Ris reported as follows:

There are in the Selys collection two specimens under this label: (1) Bears a label with *aurantiaca* canceled and *crocea* written in Selys's hand, and a second label with *paucinervis* alone. This specimen is clearly different from Mr. Williamson's specimen

[1] See Calvert, Biologia Centrali-Americana, Odonata, p. 143, April, 1903.

aurantiaca from Los Amates. (2) *P. aurantiaca*, Panama, 2 green labels; this specimen is certainly Mr. Williamson's species, though having the black bands of the thorax somewhat narrower; the appendages are the same.

The female of *aurantiaca*, not previously known, is described below.

Length of abdomen, female, 27 mm.; hind wing, female, 18 mm.

Head similar to male, with the following exceptions: Pale areas in front slightly more extensive, the labrum with the lower third pale, not entirely black as in the male. The geminate orange spot on the dorsum of the frons at its anterior edge in the male is entirely wanting in the female. Thoracic markings similar in the two sexes, but the dark markings more extensive in the female; especially true of the middorsal stripe, which is about twice as wide as in the male. In the female, as might be expected, the pale colors are less brilliant, especially on the lower part of the thorax and the legs. No mesostigmal spine.

Abdomen black above, a narrow basal ring on 3; 1–7 with sides above dark and lower half pale; 3 and 4 apically encircled with dark; 8 and 9 each with a lateral pale spot; 10 black. Genital valves reaching the end of 10, the long slender palpi exceeding the conical short appendages which are shorter than 10.

PROTONEURA CAPILLARIS Rambur.

This, the type of *Protoneura*, is found only in Cuba, where no other species of the genus are known to occur; mesepisternum and mesepimeron (the latter not entirely in the young) black or violet-black; male abdomen with segment 3 about five times as long as 2, and the basal fourth dorsally blue; 4–6 with pale basal rings; 7 blue with an apical brown ring; 8–10 black, a little yellow on the sides; female abdomen bronze black, 3–7 with pale basal rings and larger black apical rings; abdomen, male 30–30.5 mm., female 25–26 mm.; hind wing, male 16.5–17 mm., female 17.5–18.5 mm.

In the key to genera and species *capillaris* will fall in b^2 under a^1. It may be separated at once from the Central American species falling under the same section by the unmarked black or violet-black mesepisternum.

I am indebted to Doctor Calvert for the loan of the left front and hind wings of a male from Cuba, collected by C. L. Wright, in the Academy of Natural Sciences of Philadelphia. Doctor Calvert also sent me a sketch of the basal parts of the right wings of the same specimen.

EPIPLEONEURA LAMINA, new species.

Length of abdomen, male 29–31 mm., female 26.5; hind wing, male 18–19 mm., female 18.

Head.—Male and female. Black above with green reflections; labium pale flesh; lower third of labrum dull pale yellow; anteclypeus and frons below in front light yellow, continuous with the genae, which are green against the eyes; a triangular greenish yellow spot, surrounded with black, in front of each antenna and on the frons in front.

Prothorax.—Male and female. Above dark shining green; sides brown, darker against the green, paler below; beneath pale flesh; hind lobe low, convex.

Thorax.—Male and female. Dark shining green above, including the mesepisternum and mesepimeron and the upper end of the metepisternum; a very short and narrow superior brown humeral stripe; sides below the green area very pale brown, almost flesh, passing into pale flesh beneath; the pale area of the metepisternum more or less definitely edged with dark.

Abdomen.—Male. Above black, the basal segments with green reflections; obscure, scarcely evident brown basal rings on 3–7; apical articulation of 7 pale; apical third or fourth of 9 pale in life (pale blue?), in dried material dark dull brown; sides dark, shading below into the obscure yellowish brown of the under parts; appendages black.

Female. Similar to male; pale area of sides more extensive (dorsal black narrower); apical articulations of 7–8 pale. Genital valves slightly exceeding 10, the long slender palpi reaching the end of the conical appendages which are shorter than 10.

Legs.—Male and female. Coxae and bases of femora pale flesh, the femora shading apically into pale brown, black at the extreme apex; tibiae and tarsi pale, joints dark.

Wings more or less slightly tinged beyond the arculus or nodus; in one case with milky reflections; stigma very dark brown, almost black.

Described from 5 males, 1 female, Wismar, British Guiana, January 30 and 31, 1912; 2 males, Tumatumari, British Guiana, February 9 and 11, 1912; and 3 males, Potaro Landing, British Guiana, February 10, 1912. Type, a male and allotype, a female from Wismar, in my collection. The name refers to the shape of the terminal abdominal plate of the male.

Paratype.—Cat. No. 19215, U.S.N.M. A male from Wismar, British Guiana, January 31, 1912.

Between Wismar and Christianburg is a small stream flowing into the Demerara River and crossed by the footpath between the two towns. In the afternoon the backward flow of the river due to tides makes this stream almost unwadable near its mouth. We were attracted to this muddy, log-choked creek by the beautiful *Diastatops dimidiata*, which we found nowhere else. The banks of the creek are generally covered with impenetrable brush and the exposed margins are slippery and treacherous, due to the rise and fall of water over them. At places logs are piled so indiscriminately in the creek that progress is slow and difficult; and at places the overhanging bushes completely shade the stream. It was among these bushes that *E. lamina* and *E. fuscaenea* moved with drifting flight from near the water's surface to rest in the dense vegetation.

When this study was first begun, *lamina* and *incusa* were confused as one species. A male of one of these (I believe certainly *lamina*) and a male of *fuscaenea* were sent to Monsieur Severin for comparison with Selys's material. At the same time a male of *P. aurantiaca* was included, and this is discussed under that species. In my letter with the material to Monsieur Severin I asked him particularly to compare the South American specimens with *humeralis*, *tenuis*, and *capilliformis*. Through Monsieur Severin's kind offices this material was studied by both Grünberg and Ris. Doctor Grünberg thought the 2 specimens I sent were the same species, very near to *capilliformis* but differing in the appendages, and certainly different from both *humeralis* and *tenuis*. When Doctor Ris studied the specimens the end of the abdomen of one (*lamina*) had been lost. Of *fuscaenea* he says: "The appendages are very different from those of *capilliformis* type." Since Doctor Grünberg failed to separate *lamina* and *fuscaenea* by the appendages (though they are really different), it is fair to infer that the appendages of *capilliformis* are clearly different from both *lamina* and *fuscaenea*. Of *tenuis* in the Selys collection Doctor Ris says, "It is a very miserable teneral male specimen resembling *lamina* and *fuscaenea* in shape and dimensions. I can not without a misroscope be sure of the appendages in their bad condition." Of *P. humeralis*, "The female looks quite different, is a good deal larger and can not possibly be the female of *lamina* or *fuscaenea*." In a later communication he says, "Regarding your Protoneuras, seen by me at Bruxelles, I think you may quite safely describe them as new."

EPIPLEONEURA INCUSA, new species.

Length of abdomen, male 28.5–30 mm.; hind wing, male 17–18.

Head.—Male. Black above with green reflections; labium and a narrow lower border on labrum pale flesh; anteclypeus and genae pale green.

Prothorax.—Male. Dark shining green or black above and on sides; pale flesh below; hind lobe low, convex.

Thorax.—Male. Above dark shining green, covering the mesepisternum and mesepimeron, somewhat duller on the latter, and with a narrow brown humeral line; metepisternum brown above the stigma, darker on the sutures and above, the latter with some green reflections; metepimeron brown above opposite the green area of the metepisternum; below these colored areas and beneath, pale flesh.

Abdomen.—Male. Above black, the basal segments with green reflections; obscure narrow brown basal rings on 4–7; apical articulations on 7, and to a lesser extent on 8, dull yellowish brown; sides black, brown on the extreme lower edge and shading into the dull yellowish brown of the underparts. Appendages black or very dark brown. The apical one-third or one-fourth of the dorsum of 9 may be pale in life; there is a very slight indication of this in dried material.

Legs.—Male. Coxae and extreme bases of femora pale flesh, rest of femora brown, paler basally and growing darker apically, the extreme apex black; tibiae and tarsi pale, dark at the joints.

Wings.—Male. Clear, with slight, more or less faint brownish tinge beyond the arculus; stigma brown.

Described from 3 males, one very teneral, Tumatumari, British Guiana, February 5 and 9, 1912; and 1 male, Rockstone, British Guiana, February 1, 1912; the last, the type in my collection.

The specific name refers to the shape of the terminal abdominal plate of the male.

Paratype.—Cat. No. 19216, U.S.N.M. A male from Tumatumari, British Guiana, February 9, 1912.

Frequents small wooded streams. For notes on identity, see under *E. lamina.*

EPIPLEONEURA FUSCAENEA, new species.

Length of abdomen, male 26.5–27 mm.; hind wing, male 17–17.5.

Head.—Male. Black; labium pale flesh; lower third of labrum yellow; anteclypeus, excepting a round median black spot, and frons below in front, dull pale yellow, continuous with the pale greenish genae.

Prothorax.—Male. Dorsum dark shining green, less clear than in the two preceding species; sides dark ruddy or bronzy brown; beneath light brown.

Thorax.—Male. Above dark shining green, less clear than in the two preceding species, covering the mesepisternum; below and behind the humeral suture to the latero-ventral metathoracic carina dark ruddy or bronzy brown with greenish reflections, especially on the mesepimeron and adjoining the wing bases; beneath very light brown, pale flesh posteriorly.

Abdomen.—Male. Black; very faint and obscure paler basal rings on 4–7; sides below but slightly paler than the dorsum; under parts dark brown. Appendages black.

Legs.—Male. Coxae brown; femora at extreme base pale flesh, otherwise black; tibiae narrowly black beneath from the base to near the apex, otherwise pale flesh except at the extreme apex, which is dark; tarsi pale with dark joints.

Wings clear, sometimes very slightly tinged with brownish apically and anteriorly; stigma black.

Described from 4 males, Wismar, British Guiana, January 30 and 31, 1912, in my collection. The specific name refers to the thoracic color. For further notes and identity, see under *E. lamina.*

Paratype.—Cat. No. 19217, U.S.N.M. A male from Wismar, British Guiana, January 30, 1912.

PSAIRONEURA REMISSA Calvert.

The following captures may be recorded:

Guatemala: Puerto Barrios, June 23, 1909, in woods along a small stream, only a few feet above sea level, 2 males. Los Amates, June 21, 1909, along a small wet-weather stream in woods, 1 male.

Costa Rica: All collected by Doctor and Mrs. Calvert, Florida Road, west of Guapiles, by side of shady brook in forest, June 3, 1909, 1 male. Reventazon Valley, near Juan Vinas, small streams, elevation 2,500 feet, June 28, 1909, and April 28 and May 31, 1910, 5 males, 1 female. Upper Reservoir, Banana Riu, forest, November 9, 1909, 2 males.

In the Costa Rica material the metepisternum and metepimeron are largely pale; in the Guatemala material both are largely dark, in the extreme the metepisternum entirely black, except a small area about the metastigma, and the metepimeron, except the area immediately adjoining the latero-ventral carina.

Doctor Calvert has kindly given me the following notes on his Costa Rica material:

Male, eyes bright red in front, yellowish (pale yellow) below, dark brown with some blue reflections above; dorsum of head, thorax, and anterior abdominal segments, dark metallic green; nasus with blue reflection and a blue spot on each side of ocellar triangle; frons anteriorly, most of clypeus and lips, metapleuron, pectus and inferior lateral margins of 1–8, pale brownish yellow; 9 or 9 and 10 pruinose white, and this area is the only part of the insect that was visible as it "floated" in the gloom of the forest over clay mud about a small water hole. At Juan Vinas along a deeply shaded rivulet, near to and west of Rio Naranjo, June 28, 1909, 2 males were taken moving over the water's surface, an inch or two above it, hardly visible except for the conspicuous paler blue ninth abdominal segment (faded after death). Female, eyes greenish-yellow below, dark brown above; much less bluish reflections on nasus, but blue spot present on each side of ocellar triangle; mesepimeron pale brown, metapleuron yellow; hind dorsal margin of 6–8 narrowly pale blue.

PSAIRONEURA CERASINA, new species.

Length of abdomen, male, 26 mm.; hind wing, 16.5.

Head.—Male. Beneath and rear of eyes pale flesh; in front, including the extreme lower edge of the frons, very pale obscure yellow; labium with a large geminate black spot across its base, and a stripe of black of equal width on the clypeus, these two black areas isolated; above black with metallic green reflections; antennae brown.

Prothorax.—Male. Flesh color with suggestions of red, especially dorsally; the posterior lobe low, convex, and largely occupied medially by an extension of the median dark color of the mesepisterna.

Thorax.—Male. Dorsum for its entire length with a uniform stripe of metallic blue which covers, on either side, about one-half of the mesepisternum; on either side of this middorsal stripe, orange or reddish flesh color without dark markings, and passing insensibly into pale flesh on the metasternum (exactly resembling a *Metaleptobasis*).

Abdomen.—Male. Segment 1 continuing the pale color of the thorax, with a shining blue-black apical ring which is widest in the middorsal line; 2 similar, with the color of the apical ring covering all the middorsum but the extreme base; 3–6 black, each with a narrow pale yellow basal ring which is narrowed or interrupted in the middorsal line; posterior to the middle of each of these segments is a scarcely discernible brown area, in length about equal to the black area posterior to it; 7 at its base is colored like the preceding segments but about its middle it begins to change to red, and at its apex it is entirely this color; 8–10 red. Appendages dark reddish brown, almost black externally, pale internally. Inferior appendages barely discernible in lateral and dorsal views; in posterior view they are seen as flattened, equilateral triangular bodies with each side slightly concave, the posterior surface not bearing any spine or tubercle which makes the so-called "inferior appendage," as seen in profile or dorsal view, in the larger number of species. The real significance of "inferior appendages present" and "inferior appendages absent" in this and related species is that in one case the posterior surface of the inferior appendage bears or is projected into some sort of a posterior tubercle or prominence which is wanting in the other case.

Legs.—Male. Pale yellowish; femora each with a subapical pale brown area, and a similar area on each tibia at about one-third its length.

Wings beyond the nodus slightly milky, stigma black.

Described from 1 male, Wismar, British Guiana, January 30, 1912, in my collection. Just back of Wismar and north of the railroad track is a bit of brushy swampy woods in which numerous small streams lose themselves. The specimen was taken here among the rank vegetation. In life it is a delicate and beautiful insect, the translucent red parts of the thorax and especially the abdomen suggesting the specific name.

EPIPOTONEURA NEHALENNIA, new species.

Length of abdomen, male 25 mm., female 22; hind wing, male 15 mm., female 15.

Head.—Male. Black, above with green reflections; labium pale flesh; lower half of labrum dull pale yellow; anteclypeus and frons below in front light yellow, continuous on either side with the yellow genae; a very small triangular green spot, surrounded with black, in front of each antenna and on the frons in front.

Female similar to male; base of labrum brown instead of black, and the green spots in front of the antenna larger and with a narrower border of black.

Prothorax.—Male and female. Dark shining green above, pale flesh below; hind lobe low, convex.

Thorax.—Male and female. Above dark shining green, entirely covering the mesepisternum and mesepimeron and the upper end of the metepisternum; below this and beneath pale flesh.

Abdomen.—Male. Above black, 4–6 with very narrow pale basal rings; apical articulations on 7–9 narrowly yellowish; sides below shading out to pale dull yellow of the under color; lateral pale area widest on 8–9; appendages very dark brown, extreme apex black.

Female similar to male but the dorsum more metallic and on the basal segments especially with greenish reflections; dorsal color narrower, so the sides are more extensively pale; very narrow basal rings on 2–7; pale apical articulations on 7–8 only. Genital valves not reaching the apex of 10, the short palpi, with a knobbed or swollen base, slightly exceeding 10; appendages conical, slightly shorter than 10.

Legs.—Male and female. Pale flesh, extreme apex of femora, tibiae and tarsi black.

Wings clear with milky reflections in one female; stigma brown, darker in the male.

Described from a male and a female, pairing, from Potaro Landing, British Guiana, February 10, 1912, in my collection; and 1 female, Tumatumari, British Guiana, February 8, 1912. The male from Potaro Landing is the type. The specific name is an allusion to the superficial resemblance to species of the genus *Nehalennia.*

Paratype.—Cat. No. 19218, U.S.N.M. A female specimen from Tumatumari, British Guiana, February 8, 1912.

In the tabulation of characters the following material has been studied, each wing meaning one front and hind wing:

Protoneura calverti, 16 male wings, 9 female wings; *P. corculum,* 8 male wings, 2 female wings; *P. amatoria,* 23 male wings, 2 female wings; *P. aurantiaca,* 10 male wings, 2 female wings; *P. cara,* 6 male wings; *P. cupida,* 4 male wings; *P. capillaris,* 1 male wing and drawing by Doctor Calvert of basal parts of another; *Epipleoneura fuscaenea,* 8 male wings; *E. incusa,* 8 male wings; *E. lamina,* 20 male wings, 2 female wings; *Psaironeura remissa,* 23 male wings, 2 female wings; *P. cerasina,* 2 male wings; *Epipotoneura nehalennia,* 4 male wings, 2 female wings. Of this material one hind wing of *corculum* and one front wing of *cara* were damaged and certain parts lost. In tabulating characters the sexes were kept separate, but, as sexual differences were not apparent, the data were combined in the following table.

Venational characters of Protoneura (sensu latiore).

Characters.	Wings.	*Protoneura calverti.*	*P. corculum.*	*P. amatoria.*	*P. aurantiaca.*	*P. cara.*	*P. cupida.*	*P. capillaris.*	*Epipleoneura fuscaenea.*	*E. incusa.*	*E. lamina.*	*Psaironeura remissa.*	*P. ceracina.*	*Epipotoneura nehalennia.*
1. Cu_1 ending against or at termination of cross vein descending from subnodus.[e]	Front	25—100%	10—100%					1— 50%				[m]25—100%	2—100%	
	Hind	25—100%	10—100%									[m]25—100%	2—100%	
2. Cu_1 produced beyond this cross vein, which crosses Cu_1 to reach wing margin.[e]	Front			[f]25—100%	[g]12—100%	6—100%	4—100%	1— 50%	[h]8—100%	8—100%	22—100%			6—100%
	Hind			25—100%	12—100%	6—100%	4—100%	2—100%	8—100%	[i]8—100%	22—100%			6—100%
3. R_s arising at subnodus, M_3 proximal.	Front	24— 96%	10—100%	25—100%	12—100%	6—100%	4—100%	2—100%	5— 62%	8—100%	20— 90%			
	Hind	[d]23— 92%	10—100%	25—100%	12—100%	6—100%	4—100%	2—100%	5— 62%	8—100%	14— 63%			
4. R_s arising very slightly distal to subnodus, M_3 proximal.	Front	1— 4%							3— 37%		2— 9%			
	Hind	2— 8%							3— 37%		8— 36%			
5. R_s arising distal to subnodus, M_3 proximal.	Front											9— 36%	2—100%	4— 67%
	Hind											10— 40%	2—100%	4— 67%
6. R_s arising distal to subnodus, M_3 at subnodus.	Front											13— 52%		
	Hind											13— 52%		
7. R_s and M_3 arising distal to subnodus.	Front											3— 12%		
	Hind											2— 8%		
8. R_s and M_3 arising as a single vein at or distal to subnodus, separating at first descending cross vein.	Front													2— 33%
	Hind													2— 33%
9. M_3 arising at third postnodal.	Hind								8—100%		20— 90%	6— 24%		4— 66%
10. M_3 arising just distal to third postnodal.	Hind			1— 4%										
11. M_2 arising midway between third and fourth postnodals.	Hind									7— 87%		6— 24%		
12. M_2 arising just proximal to fourth postnodal.	Hind			1— 4%	6— 50%					1— 12%				2— 33%
13. M_2 arising at fourth postnodal.	Front			1— 4%						1— 12%	20— 90%			
	Hind	25—100%	9— 90%	23— 92%	6— 50%	6—100%	4—100%	1—100%			[l]2— 9%	13— 52%	2—100%	
14. M_2 arising just distal to fourth postnodal.	Front								2— 25%					
15. M_2 arising midway between fourth and fifth postnodals.	Hind		1— 10%											
16. M_2 arising just proximal to fifth postnodal.	Front	1— 4%		1— 4%	6— 50%	5— 83%								
17. M_2 arising at fifth postnodal.	Front	23— 92%	10—100%	22— 88%	6— 50%	1— 16%	4—100%	1—100%	6— 75%	6— 75%	[l]2— 9%	7— 28%		6—100%
18. M_2 arising just distal to fifth postnodal.	Front	1— 4%												
19. M_2 arising midway between fifth and sixth postnodals.	Front			1— 4%								2— 8%		
20. M_2 arising just proximal to sixth postnodal.	Front									1— 12%				

21. M_2 arising at sixth postnodal.	Front											15= 60%	2=100%	
22. M_2 arising just proximal to seventh postnodal.	Front											1= 4%		
23. M_{1a} arising at sixth postnodal.	Front									1= 12%				
	Hind			2= 8%					8=100%		4= 18%	5= 20%		6=100%
24. M_{1a} arising at seventh postnodal.	Front		1= 10%	2= 8%	1= 8%	2= 33%			8=100%	3= 37%	8= 36%	2= 8%		3= 50%
	Hind	1= 4%	3= 33%	9= 36%	6= 50%	6=100%	4=100%	1=100%			18= 81%	15= 60%	1= 50%	
25. M_{1a} arising at eighth postnodal.	Front	4= 16%	8= 80%	10= 40%	9= 75%	4= 66%	2= 50%	1=100%		4= 50%	14= 63%	14= 56%		3= 50%
	Hind	18= 72%	6= 66%	14= 56%	5= 42%							5= 20%	1= 50%	
26. M_{1a} arising at ninth postnodal.	Front	17= 68%	1= 10%	13= 52%	2= 16%		2= 50%					6= 24%	2=100%	
	Hind	6= 24%			1= 8%									
27. M_{1a} arising at tenth postnodal.	Front	4= 16%										3= 12%		
28. M_3 ending under stigma [b]	Front										6= 27%	8= 32%	2=100%	6=100%
	Hind											9= 36%	2=100%	
29. M_3 ending distal to level of stigma.	Front	25=100%	10=100%	25=100%	12=100%	5=100%	4=100%	1=100%	8=100%	8=100%	16= 72%	17= 68%		
	Hind	25=100%	10=100%	25=100%	12=100%	6=100%	4=100%	1=100%	8=100%	8=100%	22=100%	16= 64%		6=100%
30. M_4 ending proximal to level of stigma.[b]	Front	2= 8%	8= 80%	11= 44%	1= 8%					1= 12%	6= 27%	25=100%	2=100%	5= 83%
	Hind	1= 4%	8= 80%	9= 36%	3= 25%	4= 66%					1= 4%	21= 96%	2=100%	4= 66%
31. M_4 ending under stigma	Front	23= 92%	2= 20%	14= 56%	9= 25%	5=100%	2= 50%	1=100%	6= 75%	6= 75%	16= 72%			1= 16%
	Hind	24= 96%	2= 20%	16= 64%	9= 75%	2= 33%	1= 25%	1=100%	2= 25%	6= 75%	17= 76%	1= 4%		2= 33%
32. M_4 ending distal to level of stigma.	Front				2= 16%		2= 50%		2= 25%	1= 12%				
	Hind						3= 75%		6= 75%	2= 25%	4= 18%			
33. First antenodal costal space distinctly longest, second and third subequal, together about equal to first.[c]	Front	25=100%												
	Hind	25=100%												
34. First antenodal costal space longest, third slightly shorter, second about one-half third.[c]	Front		10=100%	25=100%	12=100%	6=100%	4=100%	1=100%						
	Hind		10=100%	c25=100%	12=100%	6=100%	4=100%	1=100%						
35. First and third antenodal costal spaces about equal, second slightly shorter.[c]	Front									8=100%	22=100%			
	Hind									8=100%	22=100%			
36. First and third antenodal costal spaces about equal, third generally slightly longer, second slightly more than one-half third.[c]	Front													6=100%
	Hind													6=100%
37. Three antenodal costal spaces subequal [c]	Front								8=100%			25=100%	2=100%	
	Hind								8=100%			25=100%	2=100%	
38. Second antenodal at level of arculus.	Front								2= 25%		4= 18%	23= 92%	2=100%	
	Hind										2= 9%	21= 84%	2=100%	
39. Second antenodal just proximal to arculus.	Front					4= 66%			1= 12%		12= 54%	2= 8%		
	Hind					1= 16%			1= 12%		9= 40%	4= 16%		
40. Second antenodal proximal to arculus from about one-fourth to less than one-half length of arculus.	Front				3= 25%	2= 33%			3= 37%	2= 25%	6= 27%			6=100%
	Hind					1= 16%			4= 50%		11= 50%			6=100%
41. Second antenodal proximal to arculus about one-half length of arculus.	Front	3= 12%			7= 58%		2= 50%	1=100%	2= 25%	5= 62%				
	Hind				4= 33%	4= 66%		1=100%	2= 25%	4= 50%				

Venational characters of Protoneura (sensu latiore)—Continued.

Characters.	Wings.	*Protoneura calverti.*	*P. corculum.*	*P. amatoria.*	*P. aurantiaca.*	*P. cara.*	*P. cupida.*	*P. capillaris.*	*Epipleoneura fuscaenea.*	*E. incusa.*	*E. lamina.*	*Psaironeura remissa.*	*P. cerasina.*	*Epipotoneura nehalennia.*
42. Second antenodal proximal to arculus from more than one-half to about three-fourths length of arculus.	Front..				2= 16%					1= 12%				
	Hind...				8= 66%		2= 50%		1= 12%	4= 50%				
43. Second antenodal proximal to arculus slightly less than length of arculus.	Front..	5= 20%	4= 40%	8= 32%										
	Hind...	4= 16%	2= 20%	5= 20%										
44. Second antenodal proximal to arculus about length of arculus.	Front..	7= 28%	6= 60%	17= 68%										
	Hind...	6= 24%	8= 80%	20= 80%			4=100%							
45. Second antenodal proximal to arculus more than length of arculus.	Front..	10= 40%												
	Hind...	15= 60%												
46. Cubito-anal cross vein about level of first antenodal, or distal one-eighth or less of the second antenodal costal space.	Front..					6=100%								
	Hind...					6=100%								
47. Cubito-anal cross vein distal to first antenodal one-sixth to one-fourth second antenodal costal space.	Front..	4= 16%	6= 60%	f 2= 8%	4= 33%		2= 50%	1=100%						
	Hind...	20= 80%	10=100%	f 2= 8%	5= 42%		4=100%	1=100%		2= 25%	1= 4%			
48. Cubito-anal cross vein distal to first antenodal about one-third second antenodal costal space.	Front..	16= 64%	4= 40%		8= 66%		2= 50%			2= 25%	4= 18%			6=100%
	Hind...	5= 20%			7= 58%				2= 25%	6= 75%	15= 67%			6=100%
49. Cubito-anal cross vein distal to first antenodal less than one-half second antenodal costal space.	Front..	5= 20%		18= 72%					4= 50%		18= 81%	25=100%		
	Hind...			23= 92%					3= 37%		6= 27%	25=100%		
50. Cubito-anal cross vein distal to first antenodal about one-half second antenodal costal space.	Front..			5= 20%					2= 25%	6= 75%				
	Hind...								2= 25%					
51. Cubito-anal cross vein distal to first antenodal slightly more than one-half second antenodal costal space.	Front..								2= 25%				2=100%	
	Hind...								1= 12%				2=100%	
52. R_s and M_3 joined at first descending cross vein.	Front..											2= 8%		3= 50%
	Hind...	4= 16%			1= 8%							2= 8%		5= 83%
53. R_s and M_3 distinct at first descending cross vein.	Front..	25=100%	10=100%	25=100%	12=100%	6=100%	4=100%	1=100%	8=100%	8=100%	22=100%	23= 92%	2=100%	3= 50%
	Hind...	21= 84%	10=100%	25=100%	11= 92%	6=100%	4=100%	1=100%	8=100%	8=100%	22=100%	23= 92%	2=100%	1= 16%

54. Upper limb of arculus less than one-half lower limb in length.	Front..	8— 32%			4— 33%					4— 50%				
	Hind...	24— 96%			4— 33%					3— 37%				
55. Upper limb of arculus about one-half lower limb in length.	Front..	12— 48%	10—100%	13— 52%	6— 50%	2— 33%	2— 50%		2— 25%	4— 50%	3— 14%	25—100%	2—100%	
	Hind...		10—100%	13— 52%	4— 33%	2— 33%			2— 25%	5— 62%	7— 31%	25—100%	2—100%	
56. Upper limb of arculus more than one-half lower limb in length.	Front..	5— 20%												
	Hind...	1— 4%						1—100%						
57. Upper limb of arculus about two-thirds to three-fourths lower limb in length.	Front..			12— 48%	2— 16%	4— 66%	2— 50%	1—100%	6— 75%		19— 85%			6—100%
	Hind...			12— 48%	4— 33%	4— 66%	4—100%		6— 75%		15— 67%			6—100%
58. Stigma slightly longer than wide.	Front..											25—100%	2—100%	
	Hind...											25—100%	2—100%	
59. Stigma one and one-fourth to one and three-fourths times as long as wide.	Front..		10—100%	25—100%		6—100%	4—100%	1—100%	8—100%	3—100%	22—100%			
	Hind...		10—100%	25—100%		6—100%	4—100%	1—100%	8—100%	3—100%	22—100%			
60. Stigma about twice as long as wide.	Front..	25—100%			12—100%									
	Hind...	25—100%			12—100%									
61. Stigma two and one-half to three times as long as wide.	Front..													6—100%
	Hind...													6—100%
62. Stigma covering much less than one cell.	Front..									8—100%	1— 4%			6—100%
	Hind...									8—100%	7— 31%			6—100%
63. Stigma covering slightly less than one cell.	Front..	16— 64%	3— 30%	8— 32%	7— 58%	4— 66%	3— 75%	1—100%	3— 37%		18— 81%	o 7— 28%	2—100%	
	Hind...	13— 52%	4— 44%	5— 20%	8— 66%	2— 33%	2— 50%	1—100%	2— 25%		13— 58%	p10— 40%	2—100%	
64. Stigma covering one cell.....	Front..	9— 36%	7— 70%	16— 64%	5— 42%	2— 33%	1— 25%		5— 63%		3— 14%	15— 60%		
	Hind...	12— 48%	5— 55%	18— 72%	4— 33%	4— 66%	2— 50%		6— 75%		1— 4%	12— 48%		
65. Stigma covering slightly more than one cell.	Front..			1— 4%								3— 12%		
	Hind...			2— 8%							1— 4%	r 3— 12%		

PROPORTIONATE LENGTHS OF ABDOMINAL SEGMENTS OF SPECIES OF PROTONEURA (SENSU LATIORE).

Segment No. 1	♂ [illegible], ♀ [illegible]	♂ [illegible], ♀ [illegible]	♂ [illegible], ♀ [illegible]	♂ [illegible], ♀ [illegible]	♂ [illegible]	♂ [illegible]	....	♂ [illegible]	♂ [illegible]	♂ [illegible], ♀ [illegible]	♂ [illegible], ♀1	♂ [illegible]	♂ [illegible], ♀ [illegible]
Segment No. 2	♂1½, ♀1½	♂1½, ♀1½	♂1½, ♀1½	♂1½, ♀1½	♂1½	♂1½	....	♂1½	♂1¼	♂1½, ♀1½	♂1½, ♀2	♂1½	♂1½, ♀1½
Segment No. 3	♂8, ♀7	♂7, ♀6½	♂7½, ♀7	♂7, ♀6	♂7	♂7½	....	♂6½	♂6½	♂7, ♀6½	♂6, ♀6½	♂5½	♂5½, ♀5
Segment No. 4	♂9½, ♀8	♂8, ♀7	♂8½, ♀8	♂8, ♀7	♂7½	♂8	....	♂7	♂7½	♂7½, ♀6½	♂7½, ♀7½	♂6½	♂6, ♀5
Segment No. 5	♂10, ♀8	♂8½, ♀7½	♂8½, ♀8	♂8, ♀7	♂8	♂8½	....	♂7	♂7½	♂7½, ♀7	♂7½, ♀7½	♂6½	♂6½, ♀5
Segment No. 6	♂9, ♀7	♂8, ♀7	♂8½, ♀7	♂8, ♀6½	♂7½	♂8½	....	♂6½	♂7	♂7½, ♀7	♂7½, ♀7½	♂6½	♂6, ♀5
Segment No. 7	♂5, ♀4	♂4½, ♀4	♂5, ♀4	♂4½, ♀4½	♂5	♂5	....	♂4½	♂4½	♂5, ♀4½	♂6, ♀6	♂4½	♂4, ♀3½
Segment No. 8	♂1½, ♀1	♂1½, ♀1½	♂1½, ♀1	♂1½, ♀1½	♂2	♂1½	....	♂2	♂1½	♂1½, ♀1½	♂2, ♀2	♂2½	♂1½, ♀1½
Segment No. 9	♂1, ♀1¼	♂1, ♀1	♂1, ♀1¼	♂1, ♀1	♂1	♂1¼	....	♂1	♂1	♂1, ♀1	♂1, ♀1	♂1	♂1, ♀1
Segment No. 10	♂ [illegible], ♀ [illegible]	♂ [illegible], ♀ ½	♂ [illegible], ♀ [illegible]	♂ [illegible], ♀ ½	♂ [illegible]	♂ [illegible]	....	♂ [illegible]	♂ [illegible]	♂ ½, ♀ ½	♂ ½, ♀ ½	♂ ½	♂ ½, ♀ ½

See page 636 for footnotes to tabulation of venation.

FOOTNOTES TO TABULATION OF VENATION.

a In those cases where Cu_1 terminates against the descending cross vein and not at its posterior termination, the cross vein is more or less angled at the point of contact and the posterior termination of the cross vein is deflected apically. In extreme cases of this which I have noticed in *calverti* and other species Cu_1 appears at first glance to be produced beyond the descending cross vein, but in no such cases does the cross vein actually cross Cu_1 to reach the wing margin basally to the termination of Cu_1, and this apparent extension of Cu_1 is really the apically deflected posterior end of the descending cross vein.

b The position of termination of M_3, or any unbroken vein, is much more accurately treated in tabulations than the same character for broken veins such as M_4 which near its termination may disappear in the posterior wing margin proximal to its real termination (see hind wings of *calverti* and *cara*, pl. 41, figs. 1 and 5).

c The first antenodal costal space is the space between wing base and first antenodal. The second antenodal costal space is the space between the antenodals. The third antenodal costal space is the space between the second antenodal and the nodus.

d In 1 female both hind wings have R_s arising very slightly proximal to the subnodus. The same wings have R_s and M_3 joined at the first descending cross vein.

e In 1 hind wing of a male from Morales the first antenodal costal space is very long, due to the distal displacement of the first antenodal.

f Distal about one-fourth the second antenodal costal space in all 4 wings of a single individual.

g In one wing there is a cross vein at right angles to the wing in the area beyond the descending cross vein and bounded by Cu_1 and the posterior wing margin.

h In one left wing Cu_1 extends far beyond the cross vein, but the latter is *not* continued to the wing margin.

i In 2 wings Cu_1 is produced as far apically as the next cross vein beyond the cross vein descending from the subnodus.

k In one left wing the first antenodal is displaced distally, making the second antenodal costal space very short and lengthening the first space. In the same wing the cubito-anal cross vein is displaced distally. In another individual a left wing has an added antenodal in the first series between the 2 normal antenodals.

l An individual in which M_2 was displaced apically in all 4 wings.

m In 5 front wings and 11 hind wings Cu_1 ends against the descending cross vein instead of at its posterior termination and in each of these cases the posterior termination of the cross vein is slightly deflected apically.

n In one wing there is a basally directed spur from M_{1a} extending about one-third across the cell basal to M_{1a} at its origin.

o In one wing covering only about two-thirds of a cell.

p In 2 wings covering only about one-half a cell, due to irregularity in cells posterior to the stigma rather than to any variation in the stigma itself.

r In one wing due to the same causes discussed under footnote *p*.

EXPLANATION OF PLATES.

PLATE 38.

All figures with same magnification. All profile views are of the left side. Male appendages are all apically black, and the sparse short hairs, which are present, are omitted in the drawings. Figs. 1–18, males; figs. 19–21, female.

Figs. 1–4. *Metaleptobasis bovilla;* 1 and 2, lateral and dorsal views of male appendages; 3 and 4, dorsal and lateral views of mesothoracic horns.

Figs. 5–8. *M. brysonima;* same as *bovilla.*

Figs. 9–12. *M. mauritia;* same as *bovilla.*

Figs. 13–18. *M. manicaria;* 15, 16, and 17 are dorsal views of mesothoracic horns to show individual variation; in profile in this species the mesothoracic horns are wider subapically, as shown in fig. 18.

Figs. 19–21. *M.* (?) sp. Rockstone, British Guiana; 19, lateral view, 20, anterior view, and 21 dorsal view of prothoracic horns.

PLATE 39.

Magnification greater in fig. 3 than in figs. 1 and 2.

Figs. 1 and 2. Wings of *Metaleptobasis manicaria*, 2 male specimens from Cumuto, Trinidad, March 10, 1912.

Fig. 3. Wings of *Leptobasis vacillans*, male, Los Amates, Guatemala, January 18, 1905.

In figs. 1 and 2, compare position of arculus with reference to second antenodal, and origin of M_{1a} and M_2 in hind wings. The differences in the antenodal-arculus relations of the 2 specimens result directly from differences in the distance from wing base to nodus, this distance being greater in fig. 1 than in fig. 2.

Comparing figs. 1 and 2 with fig. 3, the origin of M_2 with reference to the postnodals is a striking character and the only venational character employed at present in separating the genera. Another and more significant character is: In *Metaleptobasis* A and Cu_2 are in the same line, while in *Leptobasis* A and Cu_2 are not in the same line, bracing having taken place at the end of MA.

PLATE 40.

Wing photographs of *Palaemnema paulina* males, made by Miss Mary B. Lyon, Cornell University.

Fig. 1. El Fiscal, Guatemala, June 5, 1909; front and hind wings, showing the unusual 5-sided subquadrangle.

Fig. 2. El Fiscal, Guatemala, June 6, 1909; front and hind wings, showing the added antenodal in the front wing.

Fig. 3. El Fiscal, Guatemala, June 6, 1909; 2 hind wings, showing added antenodal in the upper (left) wing.

PLATE 41.

Wing photographs.

Fig. 1. *Protoneura calverti*, male, Potaro Landing, British Guiana, February 10, 1912.

Fig. 2. *Protoneura corculum*, male, Morales, Guatemala, May 21, 1909.

Fig. 3. *Protoneura amatoria*, male, Puerto Barrios, Guatemala, March 6, 1905.

Fig. 4. *Protoneura aurantiaca*, male, Los Amates, Guatemala, June 21, 1909.

Fig. 5. *Protoneura cara*, male, Agua Caliente, Dept. Santa Rosa, Guatemala, June 2, 1909.

PLATE 42.

Wing photographs.

Fig. 6. *Protoneura capillaris*, male, Cuba, collected by C. L. Wright, Coll. Acad. Nat. Sci., Philadelphia.

Fig. 7. *Epipleoneura fuscaenea*, male, Wismar, British Guiana, January 31, 1912.

Fig. 8. *Epipleoneura incusa*, male, Tumatumari, British Guiana, February 5, 1912.

Fig. 9. *Psaironeura remissa*, male, Los Amates, Guatemala, June 21, 1909.

Fig. 10. *Epipotoneura nehalennia*, female, Tumatumari, British Guiana, February 9, 1912.

PLATE 43.

Diagrams to show thoracic color pattern.

Figs. 11 and 12. *Protoneura calverti*, male and female.

Figs. 13 and 14. *Protoneura corculum*, male and female.

Figs. 15 and 16. *Protoneura amatoria*, male and female.

Fig. 17. *Protoneura aurantiaca*, male.

Fig. 18. *Protoneura cupida*, male.

Fig. 19. *Protoneura cara*, male.

Fig. 20. *Epipleoneura incusa*, male.

Fig. 21. *Psaironeura cerasina*, male.

Fig. 22. *Epipotoneura nehalennia*, male.

PLATE 44.

Profile and dorsal views of male appendages, all drawn to same scale.

Figs. 23 and 24. *Protoneura calverti*, type, Tumatumari, British Guiana, February 8, 1912.

Figs. 25 and 26. *Epipleoneura lamina*, type, Wismar, British Guiana, January 30, 1912.

Figs. 27 and 28. *Epipleoneura incusa*, type, Rockstone, British Guiana, February 1, 1912.

Figs. 29 and 30. *Epipleoneura fuscaenea*, type, Wismar, British Guiana, January 31, 1912.

Figs. 31 and 32. *Psaironeura cerasina*, type, Wismar, British Guiana, January 30, 1912.

Figs. 33 and 34. *Epipotoneura nehalennia*, type, Potaro Landing, British Guiana, February 10, 1912.

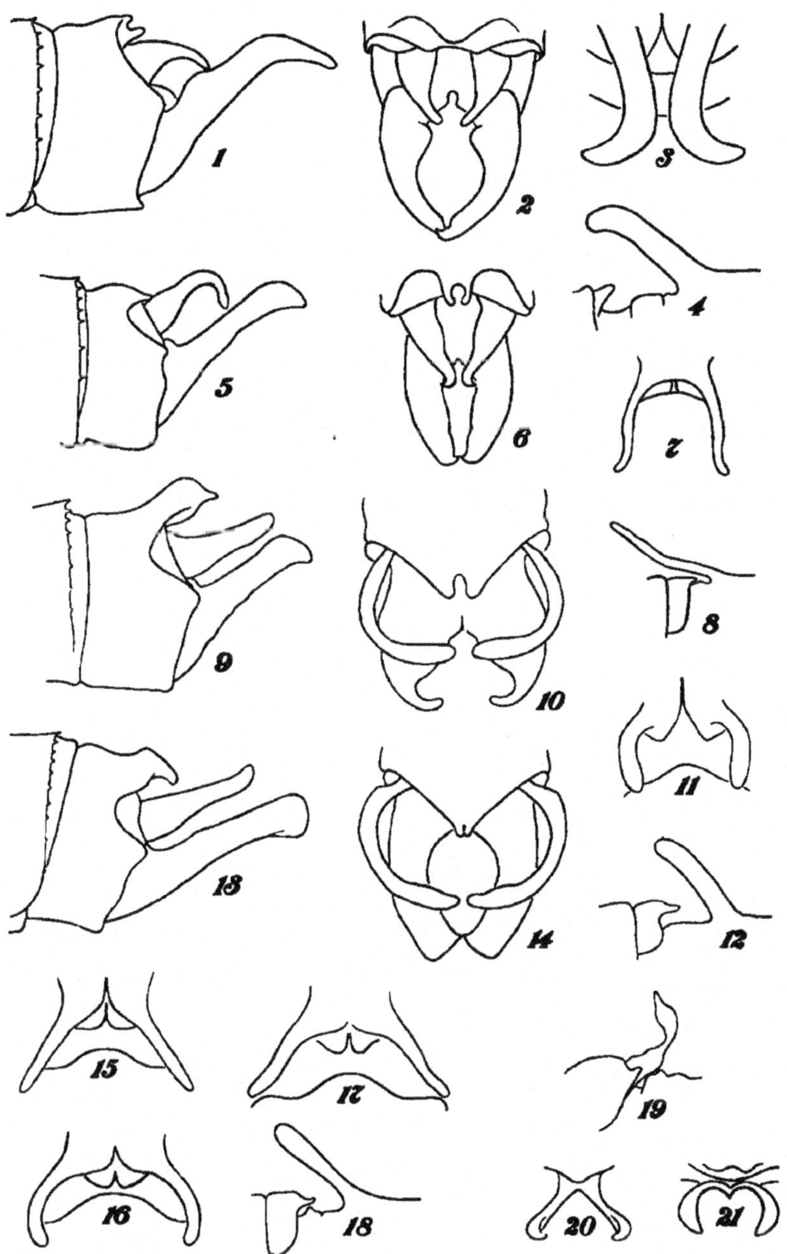

ANATOMICAL DETAILS OF METALEPTOBASIS.

FOR EXPLANATION OF PLATE SEE PAGE 637.

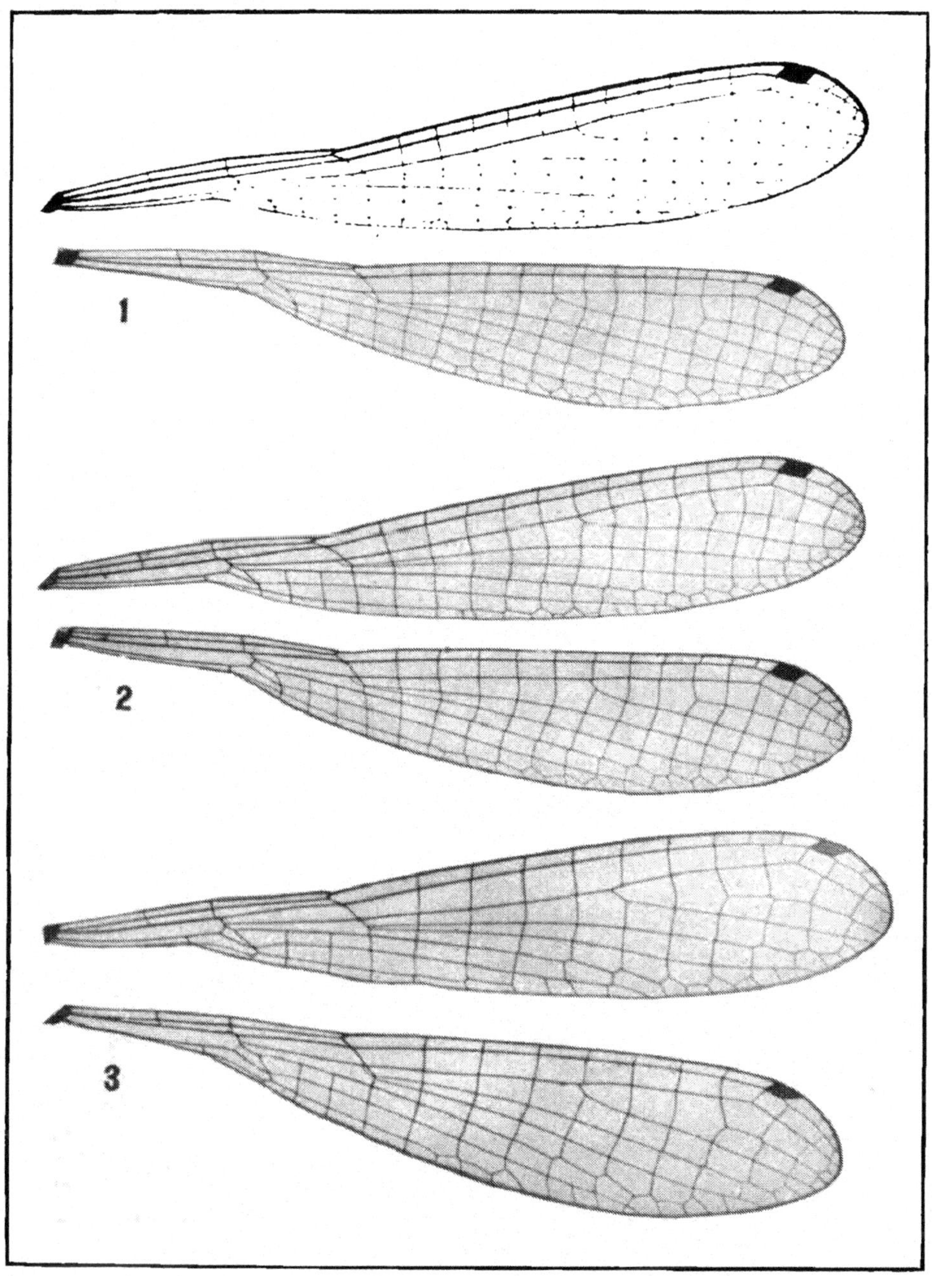

WING PHOTOGRAPHS OF LEPTOBASIS AND METALEPTOBASIS.

FOR EXPLANATION OF PLATE SEE PAGE 637.

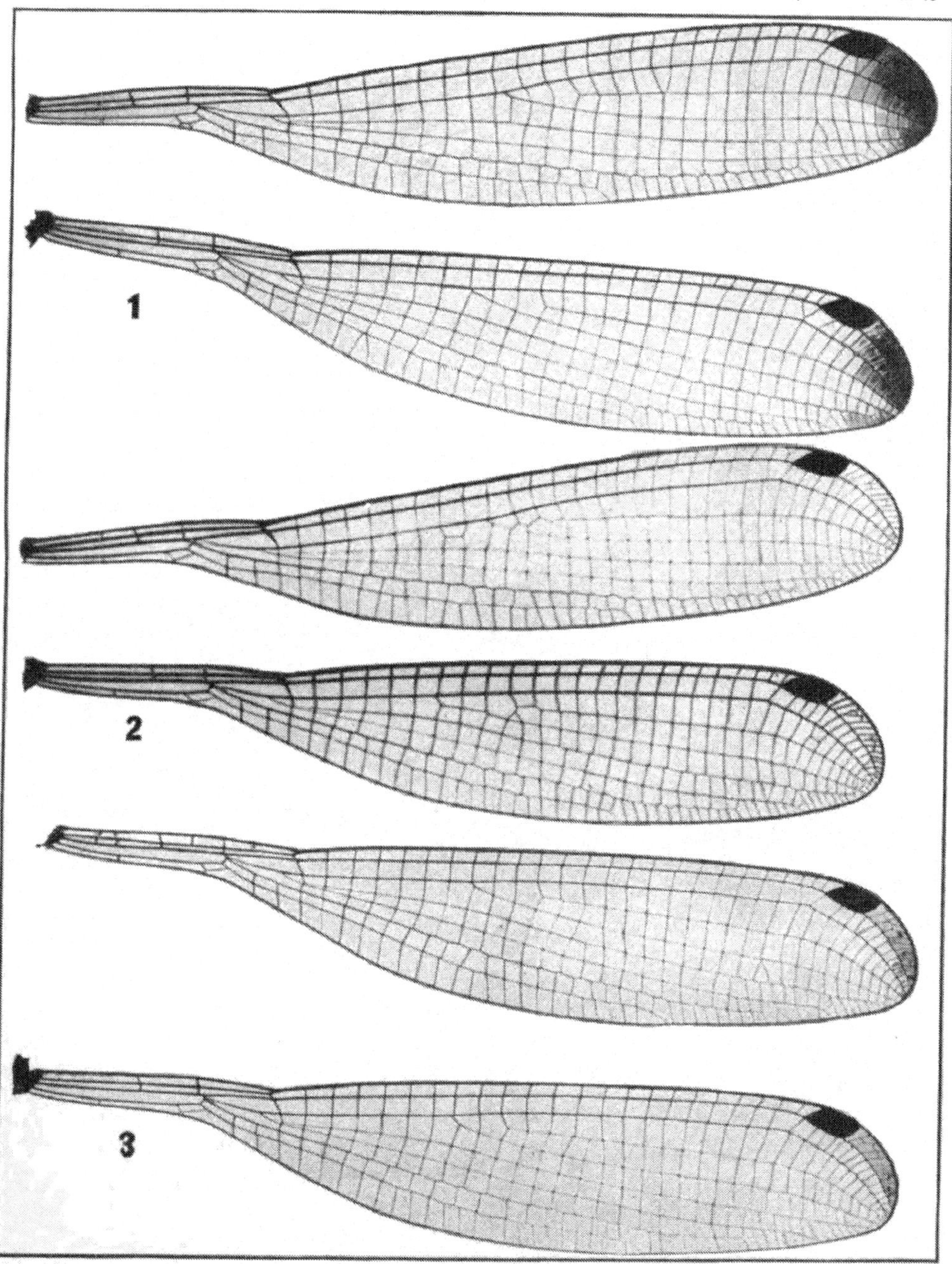

WING PHOTOGRAPHS OF PALAEMNEMA.

FOR EXPLANATION OF PLATE SEE PAGE 637.

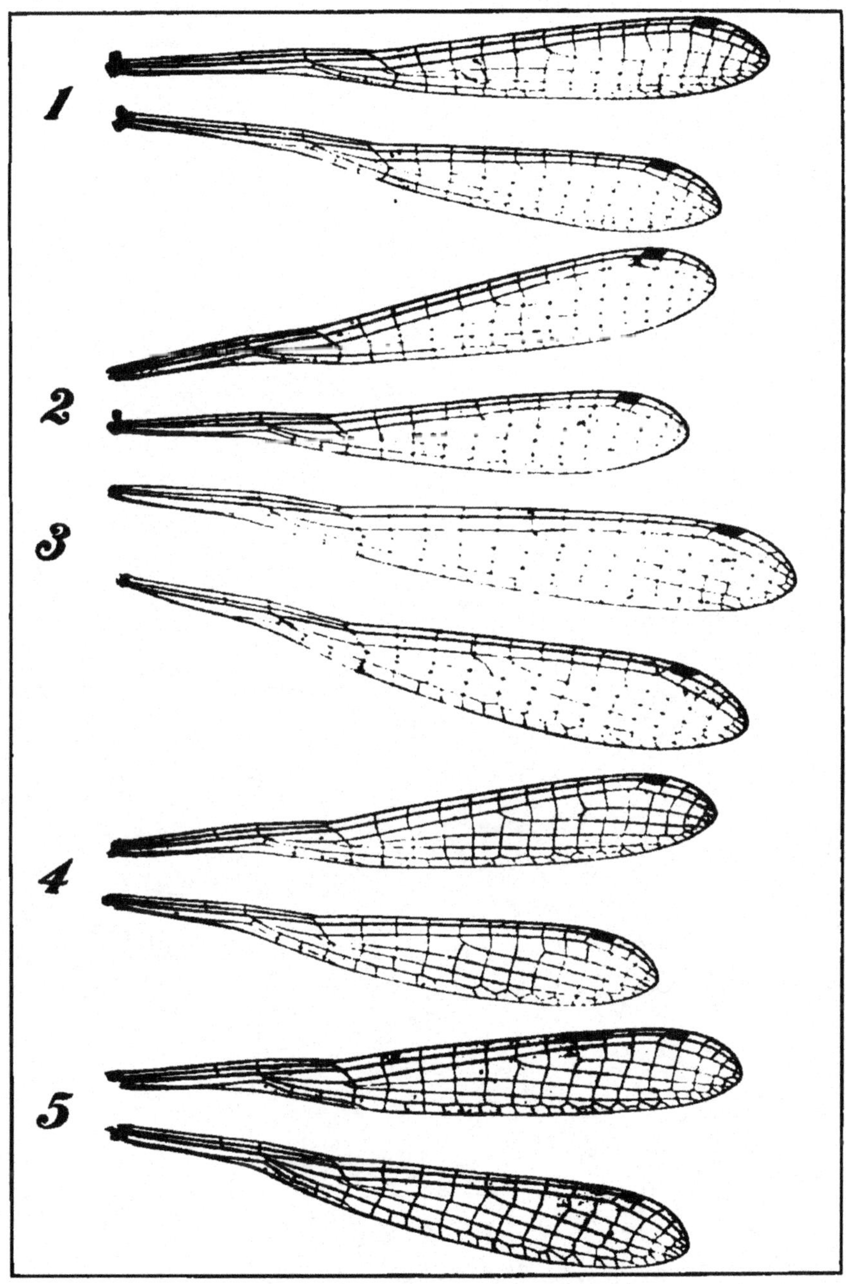

WING PHOTOGRAPHS OF PROTONEURA.

FOR EXPLANATION OF PLATE SEE PAGE 637.

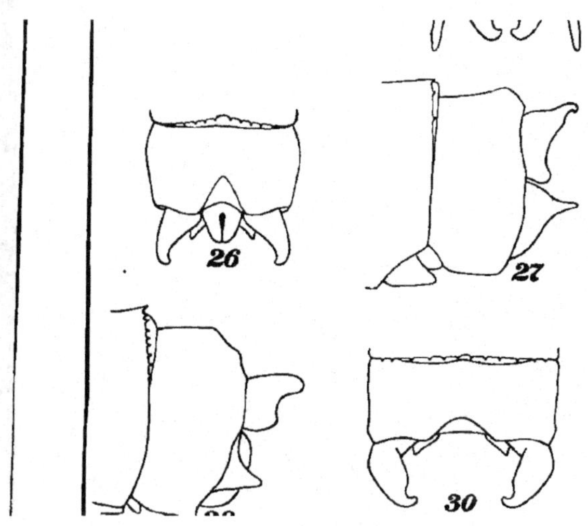

26
27
30

CPSIA information can be obtained
at www.ICGtesting.com
Printed in the USA
LVOW03s1324040416
482077LV00018B/357/P